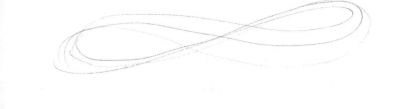

DOING THE THING

Dear Eli ...
You are divine!
Being with you is
Heaven on Earth.
Do The Thing with ♡,
Dana

DOING THE THING

How Finding Your SHINE Will BRIGHTEN Our World.

Dana E. Quade

Do The Thing Publishing, LLC

Published by Do The Thing Publishing, LLC
1600B SW Dash Point Rd PMB93
Federal Way, Washington 89023

Editor: Val Dumond
Cover & Interior Design: Al and Virginia Abbott
Cover & Interior Art: Dana E. Quade
Author Photo: Gayle Rieber
Photo Styling: Nadia Moore

This book contains the ideas, opinions and experiences of the author. It is not meant as professional advice. Use only what serves in your best interest.

Library of Congress Cataloging-in-Publication Data
2009935012
ISBN 978-0-692-00168-4

ATTENTION: SCHOOLS AND BUSINESSES
These books are available at quantity discounts with bulk purchase for educational, business or sales promotional use, fund-raising or gift giving. For more information contact:
Do The Thing Publishing, 1600B SW Dash Point Rd PMB93
Federal Way, Washington 98023, or call (253)839-8247.

To You

CONTENTS

PREFACE

I l o v e y o u. Your mind may be suspiciously asking, "How can this be? You don't even know me!" I do know you. We are all connected. I know it is real because *I f e e l it.* It is feeling this very connection between us that inspired me to write to you. Please take it to your heart. I do not always feel this way, but it is happening more often as I learn how to Do The Thing. This book is my way of sharing that exciting phenomenon with you. Doing The Thing results in an inspired sense of well-being and hope for you, me, and our world. This vision of hope is what I want to convey in writing these words.

Your greatest gift will be receiving a message that somehow enlivens your spirit to question, uncover and express the *real* you. As you do this, you will grow to love yourself unconditionally, creating a love that will expand from the inside out, to touch us all. This is how being you and Doing The Thing can save the day for everyone.

INTRODUCTION

This book and its main idea of Doing The Thing are here to remind you of your inherent brilliance and peaceful power. This is the essence of who you are. With gentle nudges, you will be coaxed to carefully uncover this core of you, so you may use it for your benefit and enjoyment, and effortlessly share it with your world. Within these pages, you are introduced to the idea of *Doing The Thing*: The phrase "Doing The Thing" is used abundantly with purposeful determination in the beginning chapters. The intent is for this brief, simple saying to become an easy, lighthearted habit of remembering that a better life is available to you and starts with you.

A strong emphasis on smarts, physical fitness and appearance is prevalent in our world. We are getting better at taking care of our bodies with nutrition and exercise. Good. But, something is missing. It is a critical piece to the puzzle of human evolution. Now it is time to give top priority to the non-physical part of ourselves, which is in desperate need of care. In Doing The Thing, you will be asked to direct your attention to the things you can't see, like the beliefs, thoughts, words, feelings and instincts that make up the spirit, heart and soul of you. Focusing here will benefit *a l l* of you. Our lives are largely run by what we see with our eyes. As we fine-tune the ability to understand the invisible, less importance is put on appearance, less pressure on looks or status. More emphasis on the beauty inside will return us to the peace of mind we crave.

Explore the obstacles in your way in Chapter 4 on Armor and in Chapter 7 on Riptides. For help in getting obstacles, including yourself, out of your way, you will find provocative ideas and non-physical exercises to try in Chapter 5, Getting to Know Yourself. These are tools that have helped me shine. These tools are provided as a springboard to assist you in creating your own ideas, which can be even more effective for you. As I have worked and played with rediscovering my brilliant core, I have been rewarded with increased health, happiness, prosperity and peace of mind.

As you read on, you may notice a pattern occurring referring to you, me and us. This theme is important. This book, this life, is about *you*, *me* and *us*. We are all in this together. My greatest hope is for you to dust off your brilliant core-power, and shine, receiving the rewards that enhance you too. As we each do this on purpose, we will illuminate our world.

RACHEL'S STORY

One sunny day, a close friend with spouse trouble con-
fided that she had tried everything she could think of to make
things change in her relationship. Being angry didn't work;
neither did being passive, reasoning or ignoring. What an impossible struggle to change something we have no control
over or power to change... o t h e r s.

Rachel and her husband did not see eye to eye and they
weren't on the same page at all, but they did have love to mo-
tivate them in togetherness. All right...so, what to do? How
can we resolve this?

This dilemma reminded me of a solution that my husband and I formulated, discussed and used many times: If
you don't know what the heck to do in a conflict situation,
tend to your own needs first. Shift the focus from what is going on around you (external), to what is going on inside you
(internal). That same sunny day, Rachel and I gave a name to
this simple, yet profoundly effective concept and "Doing The
Thing" was born. Here is how it helped Rachel.

She took a deep breath and a step back from the pro-
lem. Then she began to Do The Thing by focusing, not on

what she wanted, needed and expected from her husband, but on what she wanted, needed and expected from herself.

When she stopped focusing on what to do about him, she stopped a pattern of frustration, the frustration that comes with trying to control something we cannot. A word that aptly describes this is "struggle". Her next move was to shift the focus of solution to the one ultimate thing in this life she could control... *h e r s e l f.*

What did she want, need and expect for herself? What was her part of this situation? Asking these questions of herself made her realize something surprising. She really didn't know herself all that well.

My friend was and is not alone. We all contain so much to uncover and discover about ourselves. By taking some time to know herself better, she was able to start answering her own questions. She was able to give herself more of what she wanted, needed and expected. This increase in self-awareness increased her self-sufficiency and independence which took pressure off her spouse and their differences. The decrease of pressure resulted in a decrease of emotion, bringing more calm and clarity to the situation. This allowed both of them to cool down, come together in a different, more positive way and sort things out together.

Understanding the principles of Doing The Thing and applying them on a daily basis not only help us to live more productively and content in the minutes of the day, they also provide a stable foundation for long-term health, happiness and success.

In my vision of world peace, each one of us starts to find, cultivate and nurture the qualities inside us that we want to experience in the world around us. This is our chance for Heaven on Earth.

DOING THE THING

WHAT IS IT?

Doing The Thing is falling in love with your self. It is discovering the real you, dusting off your powerful core and loving yourself unconditionally. As your love grows and enriches your life, it will spill over to the rest of us, enabling, promoting and propagating a collective health and harmony. In the airplane of life, it starts with you putting on your oxygen mask first before helping others with theirs and expanding this concept to a daily attitude. What are your deep-down needs? Are they being met?

Doing The Thing is about refocusing on solving your own problems every time you want someone else or something to change. It is about being your own teacher and student. One day you will look at yourself as your best role model, inadvertently making a happier world for everyone. The five-year-old version of Do The Thing is: Pick up your own mess and don't tell your brother what to do with his.

DOING THE THING

DOING THE THING =

- shifting focus from what is going on around you to what is going on inside you.
- looking to yourself and your inherent wisdom for answers instead of looking all around you.
- getting to know yourself better, expressing yourself in your own way, at your own pace.
- caring about yourself and caring about others with out caring what others think about you.
- caring enough to find ways to enhance and nurture yourself, thus feeding your soul.
- self-love, self-respect and honesty.
- being genuine.
- trusting that there is a universal plan unfolding right now for your absolute well-being.
- believing in and encouraging yourself.
- respecting yourself so much that you do not allow anyone to disrespect you.
- no longer trying to fix what is not yours to fix. Living gets easier as we accept that each of us has our own path of growth and evolution. What an intrusion when we tell each other what to do with that path.

- celebrating who you are. You may first need to re-discover who you really are to remember what you have to celebrate.
- giving yourself what you think you need from others, like love, security or approval.
- accepting what you are responsible for and stop blaming. This retrieves the power that blaming gives away. If you are frustrated with your kids, boss, spouse, neighbor or world, the feeling of frustration is not really about them.

  It is about you. The good news is, when you start from the inside out, you work from a place of pure potential because you are working with the divine source of power in you. This is the one source you can rely on for anything.
- not playing the victim. You cannot change others, but you can change how they treat you by taking responsibility for your part of events, getting your power back and doing what ever you need to do to take care of yourself. After long-time patterns have formed, this can take tremendous

courage. It may only work if you are prepared to

say goodbye to a relationship that is not healthy.

- asking yourself "what part do I play in this...

problem, conflict or situation?"

In conflict with others, you may be tempted to ask, "What is *their* problem?" The solution lies instead in asking, "What is *my* part in this conflict? What is *my* problem?" asked with the utmost self-respect and non-judgment; this is not to say that others do not have problems. It is about focusing your energy where you have potential to use it, with yourself. It takes at least two people to have an interpersonal conflict. So if you are in a conflict, you are partly responsible for it. You have no constructive power over others here, but you do have ultimate influence with yourself. When you stop blaming, solutions eventually come. They are substantial answers that help you gain more access to your power. Talking about Doing The Thing with power is not intended to fuel a power trip. Take into consideration the vastly wide range of upbringing each of us has received. Doing The Thing always offers the highest regard for the individual soul's enhancement. It is not meant to be used by the ego for negativity in any way.

DOING THE THING

Advanced Doing The Thing is knowing that your thoughts and feelings lead to your words and actions, which have consequences. Most important, you have choices. You can choose to take responsibility or not. What you send out comes back. The kind of energy that radiates from you equals the kind of energy that is drawn to you.

What you think

and say

and do

comes back to you.

Advanced Doing The Thing is accepting a high level of responsibility. For example, if you accuse someone of manipulating you, take responsibility for being manipulated. What is in you that attracts and allows this to happen? Remember you have choices. Blaming others for doing something to you implies that you are a victim of their behavior. You can choose to take your power back and ask, "What is my part in this?" Which position holds the greatest potential for personal empowerment and success? It takes courage and openness to see this level of truth and be willing to grow. Is it worth it? Yes!

Here is another example of Advanced Doing The Thing: You do not like a person's behavior and you cannot change them, but you can use your power of imagination to envision them at their optimum. When you do this, your perception shifts. You are now relating to this person on a positive level instead of negative. How might this affect how they respond to you now? I have seen amazing results just by doing this. Consider how a President who views the enemy as evil and unapproachable, will likely make decisions based on fear possibly leading to war, while a President without such fear is likely to provide potential for open communication possibly leading to peaceful solutions.

We have a much greater chance for our surroundings to change for the better when we picture things as we want them to be as opposed to dwelling on how they are right now. These visions spark beautiful solutions and help create a new world.

WHY DO THE THING?

Doing The Thing solves problems. It makes life simpler and easier. You can save time, money, and frustration by Doing The Thing. In a booming age of technology and enlightenment, you have so much at your disposal. It is not enough to evolve. You still need to take out the trash. The world is a mess. One person can make a difference by starting with their own mess and learning the value of personal growth and balance.

Falling in love with and romancing yourself will help you feel good. Feeling better about yourself gives you the motivation to uncover your glory and start to recognize how complete you are. Ultimately, you realize that you have everything you need inside, at least the potential to meet your needs and wants. As you feel more whole, the ego calms down. You do not feel the need to spend so much time rushing around spending money on stuff, chasing love, or ladder climbing.

The frustration comes when, after acquiring the material things,--that prized job or coveted love object,--the longing for more is still there. Ego and longing are only temporarily satisfied. Eventually the money and time go away. Do you want to die in this rat race?

The only way to stop this exhausting cycle is to find ways of *internal* satisfaction that are real and lasting. This means lifestyle choices from the inside out. When you stop trying to fill the holes of a needy ego, you also stop feeding external greed machines that thrive on deficiency. How might it change your life if you no longer need to live up to an image of the Joneses?

By taking the time to build an internal foundation of contentment, you are setting the stage for anything your heart desires. You will see peace around you as you find it inside yourself. There is no better investment of time, energy and money than to Do The Thing for you. As you do, your children, family, friends, co-workers, community, country and planet will benefit too.

YOU KNOW IT'S TIME TO DO THE THING WHEN...

- your life has room for improvement.
- you are unhappy or unhealthy.

- you feel struggles inside yourself or around you.
- you mistreat yourself and allow others to mistreat you.
- you try to control situations or people.
- you are negatively affected by others.
- you are all worked up over someone else's problem.
- you take your frustrations out on others.
- you try desperately to get something across to someone and they just don't get it.
- you find yourself nagging or complaining.
- you feel sorry for yourself or think, "What have you done for me lately?"
- you find yourself saying to others, "You know what you should do is…"
- you want someone else to change.
- you do something just for the recognition.
- you expect recognition and it does not come.
- a friend or loved one is sick or in trouble and you want to fix things.

When you are caught up in the problems and struggles of another, you can offer to help, but ultimately it is their opportunity to overcome this challenge. It does not benefit them for you to sink into their drama; it only doubles. You can be very helpful by staying as detached as possible. You still care. In Doing The Thing, you calm down and trust them to find solutions within themselves. Now, when they look at you, they see a calming, confident friend who believes in them.

Here is when you need to Do The Thing the most: when you find yourself saying, "What is wrong with my kids, spouse, friends, neighbors, co-workers and planet?" Do The Thing and the rest will come along.

Doing The Thing is a wonderful paradox, in that it means living each day to enhance your well-being, not trying to affect those around you. While doing this, you are most definitely affecting the world around you in a positive way-- without even trying.

H O W   D O   I   D O   I T ?

The remainder of the book is dedicated to this noble cause. As you read on, each chapter aims to add a piece to the puzzle of the real you. As you add these pieces, you are learning to Do The Thing. Embark on the exciting journey of getting to know who you really are. Take an active interest. What might be in the way of the optimum you? You will be encouraged to uncover, re-find and refine your shine. Love the soul in your body and the amazing body housing your beautiful soul. Accept. Forgive. Surrender. And finally, simply be able to just be you.

It is recommended that this process becomes one of trial and error, with mistakes viewed as useful tools for learning. Especially effective is a deep understanding that it is okay to fail. When mistakes and failures are viewed as valuable tools for learning and personal progress, the process of growth accelerates. Tolerance of these helps with self-forgiveness. Self-forgiveness is a key component in happiness.

HOW DO I DO IT?

Here is how it works. You are interacting with your child, spouse, friend or co-worker. A conflict arises and you handle it poorly, or they do. After accepting this, forgive yourself or them. Patch up your part of it. Apologize. Problem solve. Meditate on it. Say to yourself, "What can I learn here? Next time I will try a different approach." And guess what? You have opened unlimited chances for improvement. Making use of learning from mistakes is one of the best ways to claim your gifts in this lifetime. Instead of beating yourself up over a conflict, which makes you a prisoner to it, do your best to correct it and know you can do better the next time.

A danger rises when people say, "Nobody's perfect; I am who I am", as an excuse not to change destructive behavior. Yes, change and self-improvement can be scary, especially if someone was hard on you and taught you to be hard on yourself. Change gets easier when you get easier on yourself.

Progress is a process of trying and failing, asking questions, trying again and floundering and saying it's all right. You learn, try again, encourage yourself and witness your capability for growth. Doing this builds confidence and nurtures the whole process. As you carry on, start to notice patterns and watch for them so you can be more aware. This helps catch the ego trying to get in the way of your progress. As you get better at this, you may even begin to see yourself objectively during a conflict and observe your choices to make a decision for mutual benefit.

Continuously try to engage your playful, lighthearted imagination as you move along in this process. As you do, the walls in your way will quietly dissolve. In being able to embrace, celebrate and express the true you in your own way at your own pace, you will be Doing The Thing.

ARMOR

Why don't we know who we really are?
Why aren't we everything we want to be?
What is in the way?

The concept of "Armor" was developed and studied extensively in the work of Dr. Wilhelm Reich. This term aptly describes what is in the way. A very simple explanation: as babies and children we toughen ourselves in response to emotional and physical stressors around us. This acts as a protection to help us cope with growing up. The problem is, as adults we no longer need this protection but the armor is still there. Holding onto and carrying it around becomes habit. As time goes on, it begins to feel normal. When the armor has been with us for a long time, it covers up our core and we forget the true essence of who we are. We think the armor is us.

Have you ever been doing so well that you somehow sabotage yourself to get back to the feelings you are used to? Or, when you are simply feeling content and you think of something that brings you down. That is armor! It is no longer protection. Armor is keeping what you don't want *in*, and what you do want *out*. Now it acts as limitation. It shows up in your body as tension, pain, and disease. It shows up in your psyche as mental and emotional suffering, or simple discontent.

You can read the most inspiring words, attend motivational seminars and get fired up! You can learn all the world's greatest secrets. But, if you do not clear out what is in your way, you tend to stay stuck. One of the biggest problems with armor is that you do not just haul it around mucking up and limiting yourself. You almost always pass it around and share it, especially with your loved ones. Unfortunately, children absorb armor like sponges, if their methods of fighting it off have not worked. Let us unload as much of our armor as we can for our welfare and for the innocent bystanders in our wake. We can learn to take off the armor and find freedom by having a willingness to look at it, a curiosity to question how it got there and an openness to wonder how life can feel without it?

GETTING TO KNOW YOURSELF

WHY SHOULD I?

Getting to know yourself prepares you to Do The Thing successfully. What does this mean? As with anything in life, if we do not assume to know it all, there is so much we can learn and use for our benefit. This chapter wants to help you learn more about you and see the value plus the rewards that come with doing so. Your happiness promotes global health. It starts with you and how you feel about yourself. The most important things you do in your lifetime are not "out there" in the world, but within yourself at home. How you treat yourself, your dog, your family, friends and others is the foundation of success.

CONSTRUCTIVE SELFISHNESS

You can improve anything by getting to know yourself better and loving yourself more. "Isn't self-love selfish? I don't want to be selfish or self-centered." Selfishness shuts the rest of us out at everyone's expense. But, self-love and being interested in yourself is the opposite. It honors the collective conscience. In caring for your own soul, you reconnect with yourself at the deepest level. You grow in awareness of the interconnectedness of the Universe.

We can look to nature for guidance. Healthy animals are good examples of self-love. They have no egoist agenda to get in their way. Watch a cat taking a bath, playing, napping, eating. They are great at taking care of themselves and they rarely do something they do not want to do. A happy dog is the epitome of unconditional love. These creatures live in a state of grace.

ROMANCING YOURSELF

What words come to mind when you think of romance? How about: Interested * Love * Contact * Appreciation Respect * Acceptance * Intimacy * Fun * Excitement

Including the idea of romancing yourself is designed to entice you into seeing yourself in a fresh and exciting new way. Taking an interest in yourself and Doing The Thing in self-discovery are the opposites of self-indulgence and narcissism. They also have the opposite results. Self-indulgence and narcissism come from a place of ego, lack and insecurity and typically result in alienation. The person acting on ego self-centeredness will push others away, even though deep down they crave and need the exact opposite. In a world of people acting this way, it is "every man for himself". This attitude perpetuates a self-fulfilling prophecy of mistrust and greed.

On the other hand, in a Doing-The-Thing world, you are curious enough about yourself to show some interest in your own process of being human: "Who am I? What am I doing here?" or at least "How can I be happy?" This heart-driven selfishness is the catalyst for self-care and love. The person acting in this world, with this process, is open to themselves and others, mistakes and all. You are learning to solve your problems and heal. As your self-respect and love grow, you feel less empty, more complete and safer in the world. Feeling safer inside gives you more confidence and strength no matter what is going on around you. Now we are getting somewhere! Being more complete means you no longer need to take from others or look to others to try to satisfy your insecurities. As your internal love blossoms, so does love, tolerance and respect for others, resulting in a compassionate responsibility to all life and the enhancement of all.

If I am operating from fear and lack, I am going to take the money and run. If I am operating from completeness, I am going to look at how I am affecting myself and my world. Tending to my well-being first is a most generous gift I can offer us all.

WHO AM I?

As children we are taught to respect our elders because our parents, teachers, leaders and authority figures know what is best. Unfortunately, some are trustworthy and some are not.

Has this mindset been in our best interest? What about attention to the self-respect and value inside each of us? Is mutual respect possible without a foundation of self-respect? How much more beneficial it is to be encouraged to respect ourselves first, to listen to our own internal wisdom, and intuition. This approach builds self-trust, confidence and self-sufficiency. It could have helped us as children to discern which of our elders were worthy of our trust.

Often times as children we were told what to do, how to do it, who to believe and sometimes even told what we wanted. Many children are undervalued and forced to defer. Is it any wonder that as adults we ponder, "Who am I really? What do I want? Why am I confused or going through an identity crisis?" It is time to believe in ourselves. Value the child that you were. Believe in the value of the children of today and encourage them to believe in themselves.

HOW DO I RE-FIND AND REFINE MYSELF {MY SHINE}?

Uncover what is already there, your core, with these outside-the-box ideas and exercises coming up: Best friend * Baby * Expert * Approval * Re-raise yourself

Here are some warm-ups in preparation for your non-physical fitness exercises.

Slow down and breathe: Be still, and tune in to your breathing. Imagine filling your whole body with your breath. Quieting the mind is a common challenge. There is much information on this topic. Meditation is very useful but intimidating to some. You will find what works for you. At times when my thoughts are running me, I write them down quickly and briefly like this: food • $ • work • sex • fear • world strife • anger. Then I tell myself, "There! It is all down on this paper if I really need it." That is an occasional quick fix and I continue to find more answers as I go. One friend sweeps the floor to drumming music; another uses beautiful meditation cards to connect with calm. My mind is at peace 90% of the time now. If I can do it, so can you.

Be open-minded: Sometimes what we think of as knowledge can prevent us from seeing the real truth. The world is flat / the world is round. Avoid assumptions at all cost. They are roadblocks to your progress.

Observe yourself: Try to see yourself as if you are someone else studying you. What do you notice, body, mind and soul? Admit that you talk to yourself and start really listening. Be intrigued.

Listen to your body: It talks too. Move it in various unfamiliar ways. Experiment. Really feel it--pain, tension and pleasure.

Pay close attention to your likes and dislikes: Give yourself permission to do more of what makes you feel good about yourself and less of what does not. Volunteer work which gives you pleasure is mutually rewarding. That same work, done out of obligation, with resentment, is mutually degrading. Take the time to ask yourself, "Is this something I want to do?" Respect the answer.

Notice your surroundings and how they affect you: work, home, clutter, the type of shows you watch, the people you are with and your activities. What might you weed out and replace to show more love and respect for you? Gravitate toward nature. Spend quality time with yourself and positive people.

Decrease being hard on yourself: Beat yourself up less and less each day and fill the remaining void with kindness.

Be prone to frequent bouts of goofyness: Humor is a proven healer and a sanity stabilizer.

Encourage yourself: You can do it!

How do I uncover, re-find and reclaim the invaluable me?

Here are some imagination exercises to try.

Best friend:

One creative way to get to know yourself is to see things from outside your egocentric perspective. As an objective observer, be the best friend you ever had. Look at yourself as a new friend you cannot live without. Finding a loyal and loving friend in yourself is the foundation for: unconditional love * positive self-esteem * confidence * compassion * success * happiness.

Enhancing your relationship with you improves all your relationships, or at least takes them to a place of truth.

Be a friend for and to yourself, one that you want to know better each day. Think about what the best friend in the world might be like. How would they treat you?

kind * patient * non-judgmental * tolerant of mistakes but intolerant of being mistreated * a very good listener * engaging * fun * loving * loyal * understanding * inspiring you to be your best * honest with you about you * supportive in success and failure. Be this friend to yourself!

Baby:

I have used this technique when I have needed to forgive or when I felt self-loathing, to help me be more loving to myself and others. It utilizes the amazing power of imagination. Envision a fresh start. Entertain the notion of closing your eyes and seeing yourself, or whomever you want to feel better about, as a newborn baby. Picture this baby with a brilliant glow of love and light from within. Allow yourself to hold this warm, luminous baby. Spend some time here. Activate your senses as much as possible to enjoy the pure, fresh, innocent, loving wonder involved. This being is raw potential and beauty, an unspoiled expression of the creativity of the Cosmos.

KNOW YOURSELF

The point here is to find and know that there was a person at this one point in time, full of complete magnificence before outside influences began to come in. That person is still you, or whomever you're imagining. That is who you are at your core, the real energy of you. You can re-find and reclaim it. You can re-find and refine your shine.

If your intellect is not allowing your imagination to play with this concept, tell it there is no harm. There is nothing to lose and everything to gain. It is okay to pretend. In fact it is an undervalued art. The sparkling pure new baby image can remind you what you are made of. It helps illuminate your true spirit here on Earth. This warm, loving radiance is the essence and pulse of you. Often we do not see it or feel it because it is covered up. B e l i e v e that it is still there. Know this is true.

In learning more about ourselves, it can be helpful to take a look at the unpleasantness of what may be keeping us from complete well-being. What makes up the load of debris in your way?

Here is an example of what mine looked like:

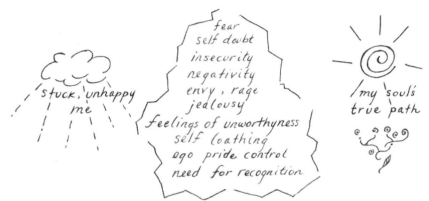

There are ways over, under, around and through this barrier. In the process be brave and honest with yourself. Just looking at it takes some of its heaviness away. Can you picture filling a dump truck and having it taken away in one load? Maybe it can be that easy. I had to pick away at it everyday. But what started as obsidian has turned to play dough. It was well worth the effort. Now, at this writing, I spend most of my time on the sunny side, with very few barriers in my way.

Expert:

If you choose the awe-inspiring path of knowing yourself and Doing The Thing, you will come to realize that you are the expert on you. How might it feel to be your own student *and* your own teacher? This will happen as you continue to appreciate the genuine you more and more.

How?

     * Find simple things to enjoy.

     * Smile for no reason and see if you notice a small shift in yourself.

     * Spend some time alone being kind to you.

     * Make eyes with yourself in the mirror and with a trusted friend.

     * Tell yourself "I love you" and observe what happens.

     * Practice being in the moment (right now) with all your senses. Regret or guilt is past and unproductive, so is worry and apprehension about the future. Being here / now gives you what you need now and a platform for what is to come.

     * Picture the pure innocent baby you were.

Here is what your new "To Do" list might look like:

gas up car • smile • chores • be kind to me and others • buy groceries • breathe and move my body • work • rest • phone So 'n So • express myself • love (as a verb)

You are the expert on you. Who knows you better than yourself? You live in your body. You are your soul. You may more vividly start to see your internal expert when you begin to let go of some external ones. Even releasing the notion that "they"-

- the doctors, teachers, mentors and leaders -- know what is best for you can help uncover your innate guidance. We tend to carry ideas from childhood forward. Notions like "Mom and Dad know best", which can protect us as children, may transfer to different, more suitable adult authority figures as we get older. Relying too heavily on these authorities can keep us from finding the confidence and faith within to handle our problems and successes.

In terms of solving problems about everything from health to relationships, you can find and refine the authority inside you. As self-confidence overrides insecurity, credibility will build until you realize that you are the ultimate expert on you.

Approval:

Care about you. Care about others. But, don't care too much about what others think of you. Are you living your own ideas, or following someone else's plan? This is toughest for those who were raised to seek approval. In the process of letting this part of you go, you may want to think in terms of small, harmless ways of seeking disapproval, just to practice finding a balance. "I know they are expecting the party I throw every year, but do I really want to do it? I will just tell them, 'not this year'." Say "no thank you" to what you do not want to do.

The next time you get bogged down by what you think someone is thinking of you, first remind yourself not to make assumptions. Then remember, what matters most is *your* opinion of you. What feelings of freedom and self-esteem arise when you take ownership of your ideas, emotions and actions without needing or wanting anyone's approval!

Take a close look at what makes you feel good about yourself. What is it for you? This is possibly the most important key in self-awareness and living successfully. When it comes to an individual view of success, we too often fall into the trap of viewing success the way the outside world defines it. We are bombarded by images of what everyone thinks we should aspire to. All of that is meaningless. Keeping up with the Joneses is an illusion because 1) they are not you, and 2) what you see may not be real. When you turn off what you are fed by external sources that define what success is, what is left?

Your inherent definition of success is the only one right for you. This is where success is attainable and satisfying. Success could mean simply being happy or content. The vital element is to keep reconnecting with what it means to you, deep within your heart and soul.

Re-raise yourself:

How many of us are still seeking approval from our parents? If we felt unconditionally loved, we would have nothing to seek. Is it possible for others to give what they do not have within themselves? The good news is...you need look no further than yourself. Absolve your parents and stop seeking. Consider the imaginative solution of re-raising yourself. Be open to giving yourself what you seek from others. Envision being the best parent ever. Give approval in both mistakes and accomplishments. Encourage yourself every day. You can grow to be your own source of unconditional love.

Just One Chance:

I am a recovering perfectionist. I used to think in terms of one shot in life and it (whatever "it" was) had to be perfect, 'cause there was only one chance to get it right. Imagine how successful I was with that impossible pressure! Plus, perfection is downright intimidated by mistakes. Allowing mistakes and seeing them as opportunities to grow is like compost for a healthy harvest. Have you ever felt you had just one shot at the right career, the dream home, true love or writing that book? My old "just one chance" mentality was self-defeating and depressing. It overrode my natural vitality and grace of learning. Worst of all, most of the time, thinking this way stopped me cold before I could start... "My dream home has to be grand, expensive, water view, everything. There is no way I can afford it!" And here the dream stops with "what's the use?", longing, instead of action.

My new and improved thought process goes like this: "I have a fine home now that I appreciate, and I can progress toward one that is even better. I am going to call this my first dream home to remind me that it does not have to be a one-shot deal." Now the impossible self-imposed pressure is gone. I am free to think in smaller, more manageable terms for my budget, my brain and my psyche. Today I can simultaneously envision my next dream home, my ideal life's work and publishing a book while being present in the moment all the while connected as a wife, mother, friend and world community member. Some time ago any one of those dreams would have been daunting in itself.

SLOW DOWN AGAIN

Slowing down your part of the hurry of life and stopping at times are essential to self-awareness and peace. Physically slowing down means letting go of activities and tasks that are not meaningful and may be destructive. It may mean taking more time to focus on a given task. Enjoyment can be an unexpected reward that comes with slowing down and being absorbed in the moment. Even chores can be satisfying when we slow our agendas. The best reward comes from slowing down with each other and being in contact. How often do we go through the day and not really notice our loved ones?

Emotionally slowing down means letting go of thoughts and words that are not encouraging or may be degrading to yourself or others. It means resting, even just a ten minute power nap. Stopping can be seen as meditation, or simply not letting things get in the way of your well-being. For those who are so tied in to the fast pace of existence, slowing down and stopping can feel intolerable. Do you use busy-ness to keep distracted from your real self? When you finally slow down, you begin to see, hear, smell, taste, feel and know so much more.

It can be challenging to allow yourself to feel and accept the full range of emotions you may experience when you do slow down. Distraction helps keep emotions at bay, behind the armor. But there is a price to pay. The price is a buildup that leads to overall distress. For those who are used to struggle, feeling and dealing with pleasure can be as uncomfortable as fear and anger are to another. As you carry your emotions around, consider how you might creatively drain the old ones in a way that no one gets hurt by them.

In an attempt to help myself do this, I considered purchasing an audio package that promised results. Prior to my purchase, I joked with my friend that I would be spending $300 to hear someone on tape tell me, "just blow your fear into a balloon, and let it goooo." Different tools work for each of us. You can follow your instincts to find them if you so desire. Ironically, what started as a joke for me, turned into a useful tool.

Try this when you have a quiet moment to let go of detrimental emotions: relax and take a nice deep breath in through your nose. Blow whatever you want to get rid of into an imaginary balloon (mine is biodegradable) and let it fly with its contents to disappear into the stratosphere. As adults we are conditioned to think of this as nonsense. We judge and disregard it. Do not underestimate the power of imagination. Just like having the right tool for a job, you can get your creative imagination to work for you. The more you play with it, the more it will serve you. Once you learn how to re-engage your childlike magic, unloading the baggage in your way can carry you from hard work to child's play.

Instead of being intimidated by emotions, be curious as to how they operate within you. Putting them gently under a microscope can help us see them more objectively. Separating them this way can show you how to influence your emotions instead of the other way around. Here is an example of what a brief study might look like: " I was fine just a minute ago and now I'm mad! What just happened? Did I take something personally? Am I being hard on myself? Am I simply stuck from being pushed to my limit? Did I go too far out in the future with my thoughts, or am I holding onto the past?"

If you stay detached from the drama of your emotions that pull you into the dark, you can see how a thought or thoughts trigger your armor. In this new light, you gain clarity to make rational choices. You can keep your drama. Or you can relinquish the holding of fear, anger and regret by releasing them to feel better, or by replacing them with self-approval and encouragement.

Here are a few perspectives on emotions to consider. When a natural emotion is repeatedly suppressed or attacked, it warps. This makes emotions very confusing and difficult to deal with.

A) It is possible to feel fear / anxiety when deep down we are really excited.

B) It is possible that the tears we cry are not always grief, but the inability to productively express anger. Can anger be productive? [Anger naturally happens when something is in the way of our core well-being.]

C) It is possible that the anger which feels so uncomfortable (that we want to get rid of it) is there to help us solve problems so we can feel good again.

The point in this process is not to be absorbed in constant self-analysis. It is about taking some time to admit that the old patterns are hindering us. We have been on an ineffective auto-pilot system that is taking us down with it. It is time to snap out of our worn-out routines and allow a chance for freedom from struggle or perpetual crisis.

THE BODY

How is the body led by the mind and its personal history package? Your personal history package will be discussed later. Let's look first at the body. The body stores unresolved emotional traumas as well as unhealed physical injuries. These soft tissue remnants do not show up on a doctor's X-ray. They are undetectable by our most modern medical technology, but we still feel the pain. People go from doctor to specialists for test after test with no answers or cures. This is armor. Armor wants attention and stays with us until we notice it. Your entire being (body and soul) wants to right itself. As you take responsibility for this and begin to understand it, you shift to a more powerful place within yourself for healing.

Close your eyes and feel where your body is holding on to tension, pain or disease. These feelings are trying to alert you. Here is a chance to listen to the lessons your body is offering.

What are your eyes not wanting to see? Do you clench your jaw to keep from saying what your heart longs to. When we are intensely focused or anxious, we tend to hold our breath. Doing so tightens the enormous diaphragm muscle which cramps the organs below and torques the back. The expressions we use in relation our bodies are very telling: *stiff upper lip, closed-minded, that's hard to swallow, uptight.* They are all about restricting ourselves. Like a dam holding back the natural flow of water, the things our bodies do to "hold on" restrict the natural flow of vital energy and overall health.

You have a choice. You can continue to hold onto these restrictions. You can ignore and avoid them. You can cover them up and medicate them. You can fear and despise them like an enemy, striving to attack and kill them...*o r*...you can make peace with yourself inside and out and start the real healing process. Open your mind to accept your condition here and now. Forgive yourself for the struggling. Release all the grips you can. Begin with your heart and soul, and your body will follow to dissolve the dam and return to the natural flow.

It can be useful to observe opposites. In this case the opposite of holding on / restriction, is letting go / movement. As you tune in to your body, listen for signals. They may be perceived or imagined. No matter. Gently move or shift any parts separately or together as you feel guided by your intuition. Movement activates awareness.

Try to imagine you just arrived in your body and you are getting to know it. Take some quiet time to do this, especially in relation to the eyes, jaw, throat, heart, breathing, abdomen and pelvis. The eyes are a good place to start. They get stuck for various mental and physical reasons.

Sit still, breathe and relax. Gently, slowly and carefully stretch your vision by moving your eyes. Close them and rest when you feel the need. Notice any reactions you have, whether physical or mental. Whatever surfaces, as images from a dream, see it as containing helpful information tailored specifically to you. Try the same approach with other areas of your body as your innate wisdom dictates. As you meet your new awareness with openness and courage, you are on your way to finding enlightened solutions.

SPIRIT, HEART AND SOUL

How do I follow my heart and soul? Where is my spirit? We may have grown up with role models who were either self-indulgent or self-sacrificing. Neither of these would help us learn how to follow our heart. We may have been told what we should want or told not to want.

Who are you? What do you want? What excites your spirit and feeds your soul? Experiment with these questions. Make them light. Play with ideas and notice how they make you feel. Ask your soul to help you remember and show you deep-down who you really are. Practice making choices from your heart rather than your (or someone else's) head.

KNOW YOURSELF

Seek daily to find what your soul needs:

love * humor * surprise * humility * nature * hope
reassurance * rest * challenge * safety * simplicity
excitement * learning * peace * growth * faith

and

strive also to eliminate what depletes your soul:

conflict • negativity • resistance • overwork • pollution
• greed • violence • gossip

What does your list look like?

Troubleshooting:

What if you do not know what you want or cannot see it
clearly? Most likely, we know what we do not want. Work backwards.
Identify what you don't want and find its opposite to move toward:

—	+
conflict / problem	harmony / solution
insecurity / weakness	self-confidence / strength
fear	safety
anger	peace and love
grief	abundant joy
poverty / greed	wealth / generosity
depression	freedom
blame / victim	responsibility / power

Now take notice of you. Find out who you are. You were such a beautiful baby! You were full of complete potential, clarity, innocence and purity. That baby is still you at your core. Uncover that part of you. Re-find it, refine it, embrace it and express it. Engage in your true self. This means taking time every day (not just a weekend retreat once a year) to appreciate *you*. You can improve your life by getting to know yourself better and by loving yourself more. Each step you take to value the genuine you adds momentum to the mission of your soul. Let us decompress and enjoy a step-by-step, trial-and-error progression in the direction of living with integrity and love.

6

SHIFTS IN THINKING ... BREAKING DOWN TO REBUILD

What you think and say and do...comes back to you. This is true.

As I become more aware of my internal dialogue, I am surprised at what I hear and how it sabotages me. In this chapter, you are challenged to get to know this critically important part of you. As you become familiar with it, you are encouraged to play with it as it suits you.

We all have a personal history package made up of these components:

• soul history • current life history • beliefs • thoughts
• images • emotions • words • actions

Add these together and you have any given outcome.

You have your life at this moment in time.

Your history dictates your beliefs, thoughts and images. Your thoughts and images dictate your emotions, words and actions. Where, who and what you are now is the result of this process. Just because you have inherited this legacy does not mean you have to use (all or any part of) it.

The best thing here is that you have a say in the matter. How you use your personal history package is your choice. It is as changeable as a script. You can keep the same cycle of beliefs and thoughts leading to emotions and words, which lead to your actions, and stay where you are…This is generally a place of limitation at best and enslavement at worst. If you stay here (unless you are happy and carefree), it is typical for past history, beliefs, thoughts, images, emotions, words and actions to be in charge. It is as if they are telling you what to do. I don't like to be bossed around! How about you?

The other option is to break free from these old, outdated, nasty limitations. Entertain, if you will, the notion of re-raising yourself at least a little bit each day.

An example from my childhood involves a "cute" little saying I heard from time to time: "When in danger or in doubt, run in circles, scream and shout!" Oh my gosh! Is that the kind of image I want to pass on to my children? Remember, we attract what we think about and how we feel. Here is how I transformed that little gem: "When in danger or in doubt, don't run in circles, scream and shout. Be strong and brave. Be wise and true. The answers will soon come to you and you will know just what to do."

Your personal history package is not in charge. *Y o u* are. While it may feel like you have no say because it has been holding the reins for so long, you can overcome this legacy and your soul can learn to be in charge again.

As strange as it may sound, the solution starts with you and how you interact with yourself. Understanding that not everyone wants to go into the depths of self-analysis, a simple question can help. Please ask yourself, "Am I kind to myself or hard on myself?" If you are kind to yourself, fantastic! Keep it up! If you are hard on yourself, you are not alone. You are in a group with most of humankind. When you are unkind or hard on yourself, it hurts you, but it does not stop there. You tend to be hard on those around you who are most likely also hard on themselves, all adding to the collective misery. We are all in this together. So if self-motivation is not enough for you to actively care for yourself, will you do it for the rest of us?

This chapter wants to help you build a bridge from you now to the optimum you.

you
now   *ideal*
                                                    you

Let's find ways to get rid of what is in the way.

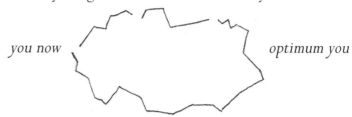

you now   *optimum you*

   Think of yourself as a research project. You are a fascinating specimen. What kinds of ideas have you picked up
along your path? Are they enhancing or hindering you? Increase your awareness through observation. Observe yourself.
Try to have the observer in you be objective, understanding,
non-judgmental and kind. Get your mental microscope ready
to briefly focus on each component of your personal history
package. Let this be in a spirit of curious discovery. Breaking
the package into segments will make more conscious what is
usually a subconscious process.

   Bringing awareness to each segment increases the opportunities to play with and possibly alter it, changing the
influence it has on you -- breaking down to rebuild. This calls
for turning your auto-pilot switch off to allow you more op-
tions for self-direction and clarity in your choices. Doing so
takes you from reactive--on auto-pilot, not in charge-- to pro-
active, making wide-awake choices in your favor. Awareness

brings empowerment. Becoming more aware of these parts of you empowers you to shift them if you want to.

Soul history: If you wish to, it can be helpful to revisit and observe the experiences of your soul before you were born. Choosing to do this allowed me to disarm the most stubborn and troubling part of my armor, more of which will be revealed later.

Present life history: Review, as impartially as you can, your life from birth to now. Whether the review is sketchy or thorough, consider how your history has influenced your beliefs and life choices up to now. One way to do this is to write your life story.

Thoughts and images: Listen to the thoughts in your head and look at the pictures in your mind's eye. Are they helpful or harmful? Can you notice any emotions and how they are related? Are you inspired and uplifted or not? Consider how viewing a disturbing or scary movie may leave those pictures in your mind for days. Are your thoughts and images predominately positive or negative? Look at your thought patterns and how they drive your emotions, words and actions. Where are they taking you? How might replaying old negative memories get in your way? Is being hard on yourself helping you? How might it benefit you to treat yourself with kindness?

In my favorite book on parenting, *Positive Discipline*, author Jane Nelson, Ed.D. talks about how a discouraged child is a misbehaving one and vice versa. This does not just apply to children. Look around at all the discouraged adults. It is time for us to encourage ourselves. We can do it!

It is time to shift from the old to the new.

Musty thoughts & images	*awareness & shift*	*new you*
"I'm an idiot! What the #%did I do that for!?"	**unkind**	*"I can learn from my mistakes."*
"I'm ugly, fat, dumb."	**judgment**	*"I accept myself right now."*
"Things are going so well I better watch out, something bad will happen"	**fear and sabotage**	*"I deserve this pleasure and allow it to feed my well-being."*
"The planet is a mess, and there is nothing I can do about it!"	**negativity and helplessness**	*"By Doing The Thing I am living on purpose to create a world I love."*

Now pay attention to how your thoughts and images make you feel. This part can be simple. If you are feeling good in your heart, you are right on track. If you are feeling bad, you are off the track to well-being. It is time to shift your thoughts and images to something more positive to help you feel better about yourself. Practice and play with this tool.

More depth on this concept and a wealth of related information can be found in a wonderful series of books by Esther and Jerry Hicks (The Teachings of Abraham). Once you get the hang of this process, life gets easier. You are no longer on a runaway horse of your personal history package, controlled by its negative patterns and worn-out habits. With practice, each component can be tamed.

Picture a tiger in your mind.

Picture one of the fiercest kind.

She is hate and greed and war.

She is waiting at Hades' door.

Tame this creature to end your strife.

Tame her toward a peaceful life.

Do this daily for all you're worth.

Not Heaven "out there", but here on Earth.

Emotions: Take a look at emotions now. They are

influenced by thoughts and images which are tied in with our historical frames of reference. Sometimes emotions make sense and serve us well. Other times--the opposite. For example: An aboriginal mother in a geographic location where snakes are deadly, will pass on a sensible fear of these creatures to her child. On the other hand, there are countless fears we carry and pass around that do not make sense and only serve to limit us and our children.

When you are feeling calm, examine your broad range of emotions: love...hate...joy...grief...fear...anger...envy...contentment...jealousy...longing...peace

Watch how thoughts, images and emotions lead to words and actions. If I am upbeat, see myself in a positive light and feel confident, I will carry myself through the day this way. If I wake up thinking I'm defective, dwelling on mistakes and feeling insecure, this will direct my words and actions accordingly.

Words: Listen to the words you use. Notice how you talk to yourself and others. Observe the tone. Is it sarcastic or gentle and sincere? Pay close attention to how often you judge yourself with your internal dialogue. It may surprise you. Do you blame or take responsibility?

SHIFTS IN THINKING

Take a look at the interrelationship between thoughts, images, emotions, words and actions. As you learn to tame the first three, your words and actions will calm down. You can begin to shift any of these for your benefit. Play with the example given by picturing yourself in both scenarios. What might your day of confidence look and feel like vs. your day of insecurity? Taking full responsibility for yourself and accepting the power that comes with it will help you shift.

Actions and outcome: Finally, observe the outcome of any given situation you have been through, small or large, whether it was an opportunity or a conflict. Reflect on how your personal history package took shape to affect the outcome. Did the results benefit you and others who were involved? Take responsibility for your part of the results, whether you were successful or not. Forgive yourself for any blunders. Remind yourself that you are a student of life. And know that you will be given plenty more opportunities to shift your ways of believing, thinking, seeing, feeling, saying and doing. Weaving humor and lightness into this daily evolution will happily accelerate your success. Believe it can be fun. With playful practice, trial-and-error, and patience, you will see the positive power you have in the details of daily living.

Now that you have done some of the gritty yet fascinating work of observing yourself, what is next?

Be Open: See yourself without judgment. Open your mind and heart to the true you at the core of your soul.

Be Willing: Accept yourself completely right now. It is okay to make mistakes. We are here to learn. Admitting to and accepting past mistakes, at least to yourself, takes away their power and frees you from being imprisoned by shame and negativity. This encourages your learning process and leads you to the rewards of success. If we do not acknowledge and accept the mistakes we have made, how can we learn from them? If we do not learn, we have to repeat the lesson until we get it. We have all seen ourselves and others go through this struggle.

Be Forgiving: Forgiving yourself is an essential step to free yourself from the past. Forgive yourself for anything and everything you did or think you did wrong. Go as far back in the history of your soul as you can possibly imagine. Encourage yourself to do this. Not doing so holds you back. Forgiving yourself brings you into the clarity of *n o w* and paves the way for the optimum you.

Be Courageous: It is no secret that people fear their

power. You can and must replace your fear with courage. Here is an interesting paradox: having the courage to surrender to the magnitude of your internal power allows you access to it!

Be Faithful: Believing seals the deal. What you believe shapes your every moment. If you believe you can't... you can't. If you believe you can...you can. It can be this simple if you un-complicate your beliefs and grow your faith.

Be Body Wise: How and where does the body fit into this package? The body is somewhat of an innocent bystander at the mercy of the workings of the mind and ego. Your body takes its cues from what is going on in your history package. Limiting beliefs and unresolved physical and emotional traumas hold on inside us, waiting for resolution. Holding on to resentment, fear, rage or grief can build up and make the body buckle under this weight. We see and feel the effects in a range from fatigue to disease. It is understandably hard for a doctor to diagnose and treat the pain that comes from years of accumulated toxic history. You know your own history better than anyone else. Healing starts with acknowledging this and accepting responsibility for it. Clearing psychic discomfort paves the way for clearing what clutters the body. As you shift dusty old patterns and carefully break down walls of limitation, the body shifts too and breathes a sigh of relief. Its load is lifted and there is room to heal.

If you are having trouble noticing things about yourself, you may need to slow down everything and just breathe. Being constantly busy and distracted keeps you from really getting to know and care for yourself in all areas. This makes you less likely to pick up on signals your body is giving you about its needs. Of equal importance is the care and feeding of your soul. If we do not take the time to listen to the helpful wisdom inside ourselves, we pay a huge price over time in our physical and emotional health and well-being.

S l o w   . . . .   D o w n

Breathe. Relax. Notice a thought and how it feels. Accept it without judgment.

Choose a more uplifting thought until you feel encouraged. Take responsibility for this process.

Now you are in charge.

Slow down...

  Take time to smell the flowers and the coffee and the air.

   Take time to savor every single flavor.

    Quiet down and listen until you hear what's true for you

Slowly look at people until you really see their soul.

Take time to feel the love inside you until it moves you to believe.

You will live in heaven when peace is in your heart.

We have outgrown our history. It is time for a shift.

The personal history package that you inherited has the power to enhance or destroy. The pulse of this power moves out from you like ripples on a pond. Your destruction affects all of us, as does your ability to shine!

The old armor that we carry and share can be as dramatic and obvious as physical, verbal and emotional abuse. It can also be so subtle that we don't even know it is there. It is likely that parents who call their children stupid, were called stupid as children. They now wonder why their children are stupid and blame them for being so. Whether subtle or obvious, we can shift from being controlled by these archaic patterns of living to being in charge of our lives for the best through:

Awareness * Openness * Willingness and Acceptance
* Forgiveness * Courage * Faith / Belief

Engaging in this process with yourself will help you understand others. Armor helps explain why it can be so difficult at times to communicate and get along with each other, from our immediate families to the global community. When you romance yourself and find your shine, you are emitting an invisible but powerful message of hope to your spirit, the people in your life and to the world beyond.

T h a n k   Y o u !

Trouble Shooting

Everyone experiences the need for help now and then. There are many avenues for guidance. If you feel the need for external help, at least consult your heart to pick an avenue you can feel good about and trust.

 My search looks like this…

Childhood exposure to a variety of Western religions
* Study of Eastern religions * Existentialism in college
* Biofeedback * Mind power * Self-help * Counselling
* Reichian therapy / Orgonomy * Phychic readings
* Hypnotherapy / Past life regression * Book after book
and experiences increasing spiritual awareness * Medical
Intuitive sessions * Quantum Physics * RELEASE® Technique
* Matrix Energetics

On many days my internal guidance is loud and clear. It tells me I need not look outside myself for answers. On other days the answers are not so clear; I may turn to old or new tools for help. After reading about my search, do you find yourself judging my "out there" methods? Consider that judging may be a piece to the puzzle that keeps you from moving forward on your own journey to the real you.

If you see yourself as a victim of fate being dealt a bad history package, it can squeeze you in its grip, steering you into ruts of frustration, complacency or despair. On the other hand, you can decide with resolve, to claim your package as your own. Grasp it firmly with passion. Being open to the malleability of each component opens windows of possibility and the freedom to play with them. Shift and mold them to your advantage until your script plays out in your favor. This turns your personal history package into your personal potential package and the hope for happily-ever-after.

RIPTIDES

Have you ever been caught in water so strong that it has you in its grip? In the process of living, sometimes we feel trapped or even like we are going under. When this occurs, the tendency is to panic and struggle. The word and picture that comes to mind when this happens to me is *riptide*. The correct term for this phenomenon in nature is *rip current*. Riptide is used here because it may be more familiar. Using the image of a coastal riptide has helped me go from stuck and struggling to back in the flow.

When we are in a riptide situation, we are inclined to fight it. To save ourselves, we need to do the opposite: relax and surrender to it. Expert advice for surviving a rip current says: don't fight it, float, (which requires relaxing,) and ask for help if necessary. This may be hard to believe in times of trouble, but we are always in the flow of never-ending well-being. Our resistance to it keeps us from feeling it. This is the main reason for our pain--all of it: physical, emotional and spiritual.

RIPTIDES

In nature's riptide, the pull of the current is overwhelming. The urge to panic and swim against it is exhausting. If you do not choose a different plan of action, eventually you will go under. You have choices. You can swim out the side and back to shore or let the current carry you out until it dissipates, allowing you to go around it back to shore. Either choice means safety and freedom.

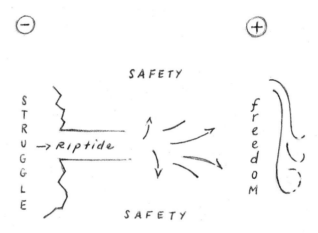

You also have choices in dealing with the figurative riptides of life. You can cling to your armor while it pulls you down, or you can let it go and learn to flow. If you hold on too tightly you will sink, armor and all.

Letting go can be challenging. But, with courage, humor and practice, you will see rewards. It does get easier. Life gets happier.

Things that sink our boats: (think of these as things to throw overboard) being unkind to yourself • judgment • fear • assumptions • hate • wanting control • holding grudges • negativity • wanting approval • resentment • living in the past or future • gossip (Let's talk *to* people instead of *about* them.)

Why do we fight our riptides? Let us look again at armor. Old ingrained family patterns hold us back. This is our comfort zone, even if it is miserable. When our bodies and minds are used to life a certain way, any change --even for the better-- can be scary. This is why pleasure can be tricky. Armor makes us think we're in danger even when we're not. This perceived threat keeps us in "fight or flight" mode. Our anxious thinking may even create a crisis where there isn't one. Constantly fighting the current of life drains our energy and zaps our joy.

Fear is a challenging piece of armor to reckon with. Fear drives panic. It drives the need to control. Every one of us is trying to manage ourselves here on earth. We all want to love and be loved. We all want to feel the ease and pleasure of the flow. You can find ways to reduce the fear and resistance that limits you. Shine a light on those dark spots. Your courage to examine your struggles instantly weakens their grip. You are on your way to lifting your load and feeling safe to use your power to fuel success.

FINDING YOUR RIPTIDES

Life lessons are disguised as riptides. They come in small and large packages. Anything you struggle with is an opportunity for growth. See your pain and suffering as obstacles blocking your flow. What do they look like?

money • work • relationships • expectations • anger • fear • longing • insecurity • wanting approval / recognition • control

Avoiding problems and not taking responsibility for them sticks them to you. By taking an honest, open, objective look at your riptides you loosen their hold.

EXPECTATIONS

How do you feel when you think someone has expectations of you? How does it feel when you expect things from others? The word *expectation* itself can have a heavy, somewhat burdensome feel. It may remind you of debt. Does the world owe you something or are you beholden in some way? Do thoughts like these run through your mind? "Why aren't they more attentive to me?" or "He's not giving me what I want!"

Expectations have their place and can be useful when they're not wrapped up in armor. The problem and the part that trips us up, is expecting from others what we long for inside; like recognition, gratitude, love, romance, appreciation and rewards. Others cannot give to us what we long for. Expecting them to, brings disappointment. If we blame them, we feel resentment. When others do not live up to our expectations, we feel hurt, resentful and we are still left longing. When you are doing something with a feeling of expectation, ask yourself, "Why am I doing this? What do I hope to gain from it?" If the answer points to things you feel needy about, then Doing The Thing can help.

In dealing with my armor around expectations, I realize I need to drop my expectations as often as I can. The following are examples of how I might unload some of my armor around expectations:

- In preparation to host a dinner party, I might ask

myself, am I doing the multitude of tasks involved in entertaining because it brings me joy and I purely want to share with others? Or, do I want to impress my guests and receive the resulting attention and applause? This may seem to temporarily feed my need for approval, but I still feel unsatisfied and look for more.

• If I simply open a door for another or help them in some way, am I waiting for a thank you? If it doesn't come, am I disappointed? That disappointment is about me, not them. The giving and receiving around birthdays and holidays offers a good challenge for Doing The Thing. The extra time, energy and emotion we invest in our loved ones can create a buildup of either elation or dread. Times like these are filled with expectations which often result in disappointment or even depression.

Doing The Thing is the cure. Examine your feelings of expectation. If what you find are things you feel deficient in or long for, like love, approval or appreciation, those are the blessings you can give to yourself. Think about your needs and wants. Is not love and caring at the core of what we all need and want? Care for yourself with love. Focus on giving to yourself what you think *they* should give you. As much as possible, give and do because you *want* to, not for what you'll get from it. As you are able to fill yourself with love and caring, you will not be needy. As you give to yourself, you strengthen your completeness. You have what you need. You no longer look to others to fill a void. Plus, you will naturally want to share your blessings with those around you. What satisfaction!

Releasing and being released from expectations brings a feeling of freedom on both sides of the human equation. It allows for more open, healthier communication and more genuine interaction. Now you are interacting with others on a different level, one of neutrality, balance and cooperation, with more potential for caring, sharing, love and the pure joy of giving and receiving. Show by example the joy of giving and receiving by starting with yourself. Start with love. Amazing relationships are possible when you are complete enough inside. Then when coming together, it is in confidence, unity and enjoyment instead of longing, lack and neediness. This will lift us all.

Here are some examples of my old riptides:

1) Wanting my two young boys to say and do the "right" thing around Grandmother.

2) Wanting to change my husband's work situation.

3) Wanting to control my child's behavior out of *my* fear that he will make bad decisions and won't be the person *I* want him to be.

The above riptides are full of control, judgment and fear, especially #3. Is his life about him or me? Do I really want to be in charge of someone else's life? And what is it doing to him? In this case, the riptide creates dramatic consequences:

A. I am controlling and frustratingly trapped by my need to control. This is what I am modeling to my child.

B. He grows up learning to control or be controlled by others. Have I helped him access his power so he can be self-sufficient, productive and happy in the world?

Solutions =

Be aware: I must open my eyes and see what I am doing here.

Let go: I must let go of my armor. If I do not let go, I will stifle or even rob those abilities from him.

Do: I must Do The Thing and take responsibility for my part of the problem.

Trust: I must trust that I am a decent enough role model so

that he values respect and integrity. I must also trust that he has the internal guidance and motivation to want to make good decisions so he can be happy with himself and his world.

The riptides mentioned are not very old. We can have both present day riptides and ancient ones that feed into today's living, like this profile of a bitter woman:

As a woman, she is still fighting with the little girl in her who was powerless to fix the grownup problems around her in her childhood. She could not stop the struggles within her family. She wanted to make everything better, but failed. She identified with the problems as her responsibility. Her father's drinking became her problem. Her mother's depression became hers as well. Her parent's misery became hers. She blamed herself for the inability to fix things and create a happy home.

If she keeps this old armor, she will stay stuck, continuing to be stunted by the past. She will also project her limited self-image onto the world around her in a cycle of self-punishment and regret.

Are we using our control to overcompensate for outgrown, unresolved burdens?

What are your riptides?

One can understand if you are not jumping for joy at the chance to participate. But, with some short-term sacrifice comes immeasurable long-term gain. You are worth the time and attention!

GETTING OUT OF YOUR RIPTIDES

Problem: You are stuck and struggling in a situation--at work, in a relationship, or with family at home. You are unhappy and want to blame--the company, your partner, or the past. "If only" this... or "I wish" that... You are in a powerless position, weakened by a what's-the-use feeling. Chances are, they (the company, spouse, neighbor or child) will not immediately change. Look at all the power you are giving them over your life and your peace of mind. Just like your Mom and Dad had when you were little. You are not little anymore, at least not physically. What can you do?

Solution = Do The Thing

What are you completely in charge of with infinite potential?

Y O U

This frame of mind is so exciting that it can appear frightening. This calls for bravery. It is time for courage. Accept, with unflinching faith, that you are here and now by your choices.

Accept where, who, what and how you are, right now.
Release yourself from judgment. You did the best you could
every step of the way.

    A) Forgive yourself for any grief and self-loathing, for
not being someone or something else. You are
exactly where you have placed yourself to learn
what you need to know to move on. Give up
self-punishment. Forgive others. They are players
in your game. This is the game you chose.

    B) Take responsibility for your life for better and
worse. It is time to grow out of believing, thinking
and acting in the archaic mode of negativity-
poor me, self-betrayal, self-sacrifice, and blame: "If
it weren't for_____ I would be fulfilled."

Responsibility = Power.

When you are ready to accept that you have full com-
mand of your life choices, you begin to see the truth. Now
you have the power to shine.

Armor is the biggest contributor to our riptides. If you
are unhappy, remember you have choices in what you think
and how you feel. How does what you are thinking make you

feel? You do not need to stay in a discouraging mind set.

Example: "What a lousy day! Everything is going wrong." According to the Law of Attraction, whatever you are thinking, brings more of it to you. The stronger your belief and the more emotion behind it, the more that is manifested.

Try this one: "I am doing the best I can."

Or this: "I am receptive to as much well-being as I can handle. What an interesting life. I am grateful for all that I am."

Your life is a reflection of your beliefs, thoughts, emotions, words and actions. You have freedom of choice in your every move. Your choices will bring you down or lift you up. What you choose affects us all.

From stuck in the muck...to back in the flow.

What is "in the flow"?

Now and then do you have one of those days when things just seem to flow? At best, those times are like magic. Wouldn't it be great if you could have that more often? You can! As said before, (and worth repeating) you are in the flow of the Universe all the time. The stuff in the way, like armor in your personal history package, keeps you from moving with it and enjoying it.

DOING THE THING

Muck	Flow
(Disease and accidents happen here.)	(This is a place of clarity and healing.)
tension and pain	relax into the day
make it happen	allow it to happen
hurry up / urgency	slow down / stop
distraction	in contact with now
anger and resentment	lovingly detached (godlike)
fear / anxiety	safety / trust
complaints	gratitude

Here is what it might look like:

Low energy stagnation -   High energy movement +

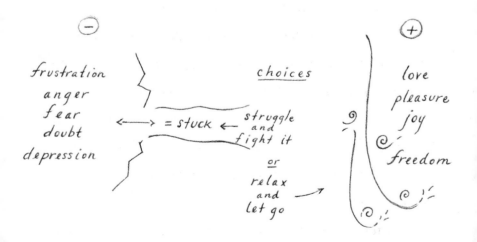

RIPTIDES

Finding ways to go from muck to flow is why you are here. This expansion can be loaded with so much charge that you may feel scared as your body and soul adapt to more movement. Persevere, and trust that this journey is worth every step. It is!

Being here and letting go of riptides is a work in progress. You can be encouraged to see yourself as a work in progress, never done. This may be true for letting go. You are unloading what is in your way. Doing The Thing with letting go = tuning in to yourself.

Try this. Pick a small problem in your mind to practice with. Observe within you a possible tug of war between holding on and letting go. You may find opposing thoughts and feelings. Notice them, but do not judge them.

Consider a plan of action to navigate through this riptide. If what you are considering brings a feeling of discord, stop. Breathe, relax, and try again. Play around with different ideas. Go with one that gives you an easier feeling inside. Now you are gently working *w i t h* yourself, going more with the flow and moving closer to your core.

Author's example:

I tend to want to *orchestrate* things. Is that just a nice

word for *control?* Anyway, I may have a scheduling situation on my calendar that I think can be improved. I have learned with much practice at small things like this, that if I pay attention to my feelings associated with my intentions, those feelings will guide me in the best direction. It is useful to mentally preview the desired outcome as well. When I wrestle with my schedule and try to manipulate it, I feel anxiety, pressure and frustration. When I picture and feel what I want, let go of the struggle, relax and trust that it will all work out, it always does. This does not mean being lazy and just waiting for something to happen. It is about letting go of the obstacles in the way. In this case, control, manipulation, worry, guilt and self-imposed pressure. Is the struggle itself keeping things in our lives from working out and flowing?

That is my little riptide. Now, if a notion like that arises again, I notice the familiar feeling with it. If it does not feel good, I let it go. This shifts me to a better place. As I practice this type of exercise, I am consistently rewarded for letting go of my internal struggles with a feeling of relief that tells me I am on track. Invariably, when I let go of thinking I need to orchestrate, things shift externally and fall effortlessly into place on their own.

Part of success is trial-and-error repetition, practicing with small things which helps you adapt to bigger ones. The more playful you can be in this process, the better it works.

NATURE'S WISDOM

Looking to nature tunes us in to the universal movement and flow. When you free yourself from riptides, you are taking the path of least resistance. Decreasing resistance brings increased freedom. Nature is good at this. There is no rush. We can learn so much. At times when I feel stuck, I picture myself as part of nature that is literally going with the flow. I close my eyes and imagine myself as a small twig or leaf floating slowly on a stream.

Try this:

- Hydrotherapy-- just a fancy word for the benefits of running water. Running water, at a pleasant / cool temperature on any parts or all of the body, can activate clarity and vitality.
- Massage--start with the head and use gentle, firm

pressure around the eyes and jaw. This works well combined with eye movements and running water.

- Be--don't think or do, just be. Meditate or allow whatever works for you to quiet the mind.
- Move-- to music. Exercise, dance, work out, play, make love.
- smile • laugh • doodle • be artistic • create
- Help someone.

You can find the solutions to revitalizing your pleasure, well-being and success if you are willing to spend some time finding out what is in the way. Pay attention to how you re-act to situations. Notice your feelings, attitudes and behavior patterns. Know you can alter them. How do your emotional riptides affect your breathing and your body as a whole? Just as there are choices in dealing with troubling currents off the coast, you have choices in dealing with the riptides of your daily life.

Stop fighting... Let go... Surrender... and F l o w ...

Affirm:

The power of the Universe moves through me like a current. I am releasing my resistance to it. I bravely surrender and allow it to move me to love and prosperity.

FEAR SAFETY POWER SEX ANGER

If our safety is threatened or perceived to be so, we feel fear. Even when we are safe, our fear makes us feel insecure. If I am feeling scared and weak, I may run and hide or I may turn and fight. Sometimes we see the hero in the outcome. More often, the outcome is this: I feel vulnerable and helpless, so I try to exert control of whatever I can, however I can, around me for an illusion of order and safety. How many of us are suspended in fight or flight mode as either bullies or victims? This causes tremendous wear and tear on us, body, mind, heart and soul.

FEAR OF POWER

Fear keeps us from advancing, whether it is fear of losing a job, losing a loved one, or fear of a real life threat. The danger may be real or perceived. Either can be equally debilitating. It may be as subtle as feeling an abstract sense of anxiety in moving out of one's comfort zone.

This may all boil down to fearing our inherent power and coming to terms with the magnitude of it. Surrendering some of the insecure ways of living makes our power more available. Letting go of old comfort zones is scary when we feel we are losing control. Control is overrated and harmful. Having control is an illusion. We tend to confuse power and control by thinking that ultimate control is ultimate power. Or, "I am powerful if I am in control." Conversely, "If I am not in control, I am weak." The opposite is true. R e a l personal power comes through surrender. Control is the warped way we attempt to use our divine built-in potency.

Step back and look at the big picture. This is a Universal challenge. It shows up in all ages and types of people, from preschoolers to presidents. It manifests as power struggles and control dramas, from playground conflicts to world wars.

CATCH 22

We must use our power to feel safe…

We must feel safe to use our power.

This applies to the very young as well as the world's most powerful leaders. As children we try out our power.

Generally it is not well received. Adults have one negative way of describing this event-- "The Terrible Two's". We won't propose that two-year-olds run the show with their new-found power, but let us consider the process differently. If you dare to look openly into a willful child's eyes, you will see power. Instead of misunderstanding it, fearing it and wanting to temper or destroy it, let us be brave enough to get to know it.

Misunderstanding and fear are the problems. Courage and openness are the solutions. Doing The Thing in this area means starting with you. Try to see your own power, feel it, make friends with it. Where does it come from? When a parent can do this internally, they can do this with their child and embrace the natural budding power, allowing it to bloom instead of warping (the bully), or withering (the victim).

FEAR AND MISUNDERSTANDING

Examples in our culture:

Small: When my sons were rowdy, I tended to project my fear out too far, seeing chaos, harm and destruction in my mind's eye. Because of my imaginary picture, I would then lay down the law to get things under "control". In reality they were doing nothing wrong, just being kids, having fun and living with gusto, which we could all use a lot more of. My old fear of perceived danger stopped the fun and made us all feel bad. I was open to looking at my part of this scenario and willing to work / play with shifting it into a solution. In the process of letting go of the fear, I remind myself to stay here now with my thoughts. I tell myself, I am safe. I remember to picture what I want and not the opposite.

Medium: Many people misunderstand and fear a simple fever, thinking it is bad. They immediately do what they can to stop it. A mild fever can be seen as the body's attempt to heal itself. Fear can get in the way of allowing nature to show us the answers. Childbirth is another example of a time when fear and misunderstanding come into play. One woman may be just as scared to have her baby born in a hospital as another would be to have her baby born at home.

Large: On a grand scale, our misunderstanding of other races and cultures causes us to fear them. Fearing others makes us want to control them. If we make them more like us, that is less scary and now we are more comfortable. The problem is, when we alter nature, including people, we threaten the original beauty and genuine birthright, thus infringing on the foundation of its heritage. Each individual and group has a unique power and glory potential to offer the world. Instead of homogenizing it, let's open up at least to make an effort in understanding it.

Now let us look at how misunderstanding and fear relate to other high profile areas-- anger and sexuality. When we are ignorant, close-minded or fearful about something, we tend to either flee, avoid, temper, squelch or try to destroy it. Most likely, if our parents viewed our power, anger and sexuality with fear and misunderstanding, it follows that we would carry this view within ourselves and probably pass it on to our children. Thus, the chain of armor continues. The results are evident all around us: anger issues • power struggles • sickness • child / teen rebellion • abuse of all kinds • suicide • war.

Power, anger and sexuality start as pure and healthy. They move you toward absolute creativity, fulfillment, pleasure and health. It is in viewing power, anger and sexuality as bad, and involving armor (which stifles and blocks natural, healthy expression), that they become warped and destructive. This is difficult to grasp because of the enormous amount of armor surrounding each of them.

Anger serves to assist you around obstacles on this

glorious path. If your true self gets messed with, you get mad. The forcefulness of constructive anger is designed to help you get back on track to feeling good again. Here is an example: I am happy. If that is compromised, I feel frustrated. If I cannot constructively express myself to solve this problem and get back to feeling good, I either turn on myself or lash out at others. Instead of seeing people using their anger to solve problems, more often we witness the unnatural acting out of anger such as turning it inward (depression) or outward in destructive fits of rage.

Power can be viewed as the height of ability to accomplish anything. When I think of absolute pure power I think of the Cosmos, of Jesus or a newborn child. I see power as the ability to use all that is available to me for divine creativity (to shine). More often, we may hold onto negative impressions of power in witnessing abuses of power such as power struggles, manipulation or control over others. That is what happens when pure power is unable to be expressed naturally. What comes to mind when you think of power?

Sexuality is beautifully life affirming and naturally healing. Thanks to sex, we are here. Sexuality requires expression. If I cannot express my sexuality in naturally healthy ways, I am prone to filling that void in unnatural ways. Unfortunately, armored sexuality goes from the bedroom to big business for huge profit with resulting sickness, shame and taboo. One only needs to hear of the gross amounts of money wrapped up in the pornography industry as evidence of wide-scale armor around sexuality.

These important human expressions start as natural. Remembering that the origins of power, anger and sexuality are pure and innocent can help us with a perspective, a model and a potential return to healthy expression.

SEX

Sex is a super-charged part of who you are. Getting to know, accept, love and embrace your own sexuality is key to zeroing in on your power source. We usually view our sexuality in terms of how we interact with another. Ultimately this is ideal, but if you Do The Thing with sexuality first, you start with a clean slate, which makes coming together less confusing and more satisfying. As you may guess, this entails tuning in to your sexual self as a unique individual. If you ask questions of yourself (more courage required, but worth the effort) and allow the answers to enlighten you, the benefits are limitless. Questions like, why do I feel this way about myself? Why do I act like that? Am I bringing old tapes from my past, that hinder me now? What does my pure, natural sexuality look and feel like? And, what do I want to do with it? What ways of expression feel good to me and for me? Questions like these can help you snap out of just going through the motions automatically and increase your chances for sexual health, stability and success.

As you focus in on the body in new ways, you are rewarded with valuable insights. Become more aware of your physical and energetic body and how it ticks. Notice movement or lack of it. Be aware of chronic tensions--which most likely have old stored memories in tow--and desires for new ways of expression. When you stop and listen, what is your body saying to you?

As you allow an understanding about your sexuality to grow, you will come to feel a connection between power and sexuality in your pelvis. The strong tie between power and sex may help explain the struggle between genders.-- men are from Mars, women are from Venus. There is no question that each sex has feared and been captivated by the others power, as history's shifts between matriarchy and patriarchy have shown.

On a lighter note, look back at Elvis and the power in his pelvis. He expressed it and the crowd went wild--especially the opposite sex!

LIVING WITH A WILD ANIMAL!

Here is a personal experience with fear of power, anger and sexuality. I misunderstood and feared these three. Yet the desire to overcome this limitation was greater, motivating me to learn how to move past the walls in my way. As I became more aware of my body / mind connection, I started to notice and physically feel the power emanating from my pelvis.

I began to see an intertwining relationship of power, anger and sex. A vivid image came to my mind's eye which enhanced my understanding. I saw this part of me as a tiger; a magnificent animal. Fear and ignorance of these forces inside, made me avoid my tiger, run from her, give her away or want to destroy her.

This tiger image represents raw power and energy, vitality, natural beauty, pure sexuality, strong instinct, creativity, nobility and confidence. I did not know what to do with this amazing creature within me. I saw my power, anger and sex as trouble, even as downright destructive. Out of fear, I denied those vital parts of myself and gave my prowess away at every turn. The tiger, by her nature, only destroys when she needs to, for her survival. Destruction is only a small part of her.

It is time to shift focus from that small part which was blown out of proportion through fear and misunderstanding, to the much grander part full of magnificence and wonder. With this process comes a new integration. I accept that she is part of me. She is me. I forgive myself for denying this valuable part for so long. As I begin to celebrate this revelation, I do so with a bit of caution in learning to embrace it all with a sense of balance and grace. Over time, this new relationship with my sexuality is blooming.

This story represents my particular armor combination based on my personal history package. Yours may be similar or completely different. Why explore fears and resistance? Why bring them out in the open? The purpose is to find freedom from the limitations they cause. The result is a decrease in pain and increase in pleasure, allowing more peace of mind and body. I knew I was limited personally and it dampened my relationships. Having the involvement of a mate who is patient, understanding and receptive, helps the process evolve. We deal with my tiger together.

Whether dealing with your issues alone or with someone, remember we all have our own packages we bring with
us. Too often we are afraid to do something wrong, embar-
rass ourselves, or play the fool. This is just fear. We all have
it. It stands in the way of our joy. This process moves more
freely when we do not judge ourselves or each other, or take
ourselves too seriously. Having fun with it lightens its weight.
Trust yourself. Trust your mate. When we clean up the body
and mind confusion in ourselves, being with another is cleaner, easier, more fun and satisfying. Again, remember in these
wild adventures it's not all about you; others have their history too.

Doing The Thing sexually = feeling safe and comfortable with your own pleasure, in your own skin. Then, when
you go forth from that grounded place of self-satisfaction,
your partner will feel a magnified sense of pleasure because
you already have it within yourself. You both win. As you become accepting of your own core sexual power and feel safe
with it, you can allow it in the one you're with. Imagine being
that creative together. Think of the possibilities.

9

INTELLECT EGO SOUL LET GO SURRENDER

INTELLECT

It is said that we humans grossly under-utilize our brain power, yet so many of us cannot shut off our thinking. It runs like a mouse on a wheel. The solution lies in focusing on *quality* of thought, not *quantity*. Like a computer with a virus or faulty programming, you may need to shut down temporarily and pick upgraded or new programs for your brain that are better suited to your present living.

Intellect is a key player in self-sabotage. How often does your intuition spark a creative idea only to be met by the mind with doubt, discouragement or downright disrespect? Many years of our lives are spent developing our minds. But, where can the mind go without heart and soul behind it? We have heard the saying "mind over matter". Entertain the notion of "heart and soul over mind and matter".

How much time and energy of your young learning years was spent developing trust in your instincts? Instincts protect you from harm. Intuition is the ignition that sparks you and drives you toward success. What focus or validity is given to how you are feeling about yourself, body, mind and spirit? When you feel bad, you are stuck and prone to attracting negativity. You can find ways to feel better, un-stick yourself and attract the positive. A more enlightened school curriculum would balance brain and body, heart and soul, with a hearty support for intuition and imagination.

EGO

Ego is sometimes viewed as the enemy. This view may conjure a picture of unnecessary hostility. Instead, consider intellect and ego as tools that are often used improperly and overused by most people. You need not maim or murder the ego. Just do not let it get the best of you. Humor and a detached, lighthearted view of yourself and life, can go a long way in disarming ego. Now you get the best of yourself back in action.

Here is a sample of experiencing the ego and intellect holding on too tightly and caught in a riptide. Ego takes charge.

We have our noses to the grindstone. We think too much, too hard. We are trying to manipulate situations to *m a k e* things happen. Internal pressure builds. We feel burdened and overwhelmed. The pressure jams up in the head, making it difficult to think clearly and make productive decisions. Ego is happy with all this control, like a youngster who is running the show, but soul is not. All this is internal. Consequently, outward manifestations match the inward process. Circumstances around us do not flow smoothly. They are sticky and uncomfortable. They have a contrived feeling.

The ego takes power with glee. But, like a child out of control, ego does not know how to manage it and use it functionally. Ego wants recognition. "Look at me! I can do it all. I don't need anyone. I am strong, tough, invincible and I want the credit." The problem here is that all this is coming from a place of fear and insecurity, not a place of grace. It is an attempt to make up for what is lacking. This path does not lead to riches. It leads to isolation and destruction.

On the other hand, the experience of being in the flow is like magic. Life is easy. Effortless learning is possible. There are still problems, but with ego at rest, you are not all jammed up in the fight. Solutions are clearer and more accessible.

What a difference! To get here is a process of letting go. It is about letting go of the parts of mind and ego that need to have control. Releasing them will free the resistance that keeps your prosperity just out of reach. As you let go, build faith and endurance around the process itself to keep you strong. This path leads to energy of abundance ready to surround you with love, joy, health and wealth.

Observe my dream which helps serve as a reminder to allow intuition to override intellect.

I am leading a group of children on a nature walk. We do not have to make a destination, but I long to. As we come to an open field, I encounter a seemingly insurmountable problem. Our path is blocked by a concrete overpass with a 300-foot chasm below it. It is too dangerous, too risky for the children. I am racking my brain for a solution. We are stuck. The children are in no hurry. They are happily amusing themselves in the background with no particular goal in mind. As I continue struggling to figure out how to overcome this obstacle, movement in my peripheral vision catches my attention.

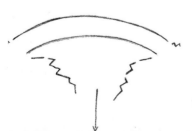

Off in the distance…a little girl, in a flowing dress, a stick in her hand, sun shining down on her, not a care in the world, is wandering blissfully amidst the butterflies and flowers. Without even trying, she has made it effortlessly past this obstacle that I was trying so hard to conquer.

This is how easy life can be when we stop the intellect and ego from trying too hard and complicating things. The solution lies in accepting that there is a cosmic plan much grander and much simpler than the ego's self-centered one. This is where faith comes in. *When you've done all you can, relax and trust the cosmic plan.* Even though we can't always see the solutions, we need to believe they are there. As you are able to relinquish the controlling nature of ego, it gives your soul the chance to grow. Anyone who has attempted this task knows that ego does not typically give up easily, but recall the little girl in my dream to remind you how easy it can be. As the soul grows, you begin to remember how you are wondrously connected to it all--everyone and everything in the Universe. Tapping into this awareness creates both a feeling of individual divinity beyond what you have experienced and a realization that you are part of a grand cosmic team where anything is possible.

Here is a picture of what going from ego to soul might look like:

EGO	SOUL
rigid and controlling	fluid and flexible
love of power	power of love
money and stuff	freedom
me vs. you	cooperation
takes things personally / defensive	confident
judgmental / emotional	peaceful
recognition and approval seeking	creative and joyful

Isolated   *Connected*

We can learn so much and use it when we don't have to be a know-it-all or think we are. Internal cleanup eliminates external messes. Life gets simpler and easier. What does your picture look like?

Most heroes have small egos. They do not go around

saying "look what I did!" They just Do The Thing from an internal lead to help. By making less room for ego each day, you are uncovering your hidden hero. You are making more room for your very own wonderful, completely unique self to s h i n e. With this comes a chance for you to have peace and heaven on earth. And that opens up a chance for us all. World peace is possible if we view it one person at a time--not starting with those mixed-up neighbors, coworkers or terrorists from another land, but starting with the one thing you can have absolute power with, y o u .

In getting to know yourself and how we are all connected, remember this kind of learning is not so much about garnishing knowledge that others hand down, but about original observations you make about yourself and life through experiences, feelings, trial-and-error mistakes and life lessons. The key for someone whose ego wants to jump in with the answers, is to be quiet. Listen, be present and allow the answers to come in a different way from a different place. Know that you may be doing another a disservice by trying to fix problems or give answers. It may be enabling them to keep looking to others for solutions instead of becoming self-sufficient and valuing their own process. Asking questions of yourself and others is a brilliant way of stimulating creative solutions which are tailor-made to the individual.

HOW TO GO FROM INTELLECT AND EGO TO SOUL AND SURRENDER

A)   Notice / observe ego: Ego and intellect are in collaboration. They tend to go overboard. Listen to your thoughts. See if you can find ego in there. How does it lead you? Watch where it takes you.

B)   Identify your ego : Tell it "I am onto you! I will not allow you to keep sabotaging me. You need to quiet down." Then send ego to its room until it can play nice.

C)   Know that ego is only a part of you. It is not the essence of who you are. The ego is very convincing and usually wants to dominate, not always acting in your best interest. You can tame it and guide it in your best behalf.

D)   Let go of ego: Breathe * Relax * Quiet your mind to calm your ego. * Smile

Try hydrotherapy = cool running water on your arms, legs or body.

* Eye contact * Take a vested interest in yourself.

* See mistakes as learning opportunities. * Be kind to yourself and others. * Know you have the answers.

* Have faith in yourself and the cosmic flow in you.

* Picture with clarity what you want. * Pray (simply ask for what your soul wants) * Ask for what you want and believe it is with you already.

Asking is like praying to the part of you that can do, have, be anything. When praying effectively, you relax completely in faith, giving up your resistance, dissolving the invisible barriers between you and your power and glory. This way you are creating a template of the optimum you to merge with as the barriers melt away.

SOUL

Now it is soul's turn to lead. What is your soul hungry for? How will you feed it? {Doing so may eliminate the need for any diet ever again}. Nourishment of the soul can be found in both small and grand ways. I know a person who lies on the ground, in nature, to feed his soul. How about music, friendship, quality time to yourself, creativity or helping others? You will know you are going from ego to soul when you can do anonymous acts of kindness and still feel good without the recognition.

Letting go of ego decreases the time and frustration

spent managing it. The management of ego is like babysitting an unruly toddler whose only agenda is immediate gratification, following a trail of desire scattered with limitless temptations that may or may not be enhancing. With ego napping, you have more time and energy to join the forces of the Universe where you can expand who you really are. Do you feel some anxiety when you consider unlocking your potential and reaching for the stars? Most do! It goes with being human. Here is where courage comes in. If you are accustomed to think of bravery in terms of fighting and winning, it is time for a new kind of bravery, the subtle valor of surrendering the parts of yourself that hold you back.

CONTROL AS AN OBSTACLE TO SURRENDER

Control is a heavy topic in our world. We are tempted to want control, thinking it puts us at an advantage. Not so. Control ends up being the master that chains us. The desire to control presumes you are not in charge already. You are, of *yourself*. That is all you need. Letting go is the opposite of controlling. It is time to let go of control. What emotions come up when you ponder this notion? It may bring feelings of losing power, being out of control, or even going crazy. It is the opposite. Giving up control can feel intimidating to us because it moves us from a comfort zone that we have been clutching all our lives.

You may think, "But I want to be in control! Why should I give that up?" This is why: Control is brain and ego driven. It comes from a place of insecurity. Neurotic controlling does the opposite of what we want it to. It makes things worse. You may think that if you do let go, you will be weak, unrecognized and unrewarded. After practice with holding on and letting go, the answer is clear. Letting go will guide you to strength, fulfillment and invaluable reward.

How do you tell whether you are holding on (controlling) or letting go (in the flow)?

Here are the results of control: problems • internal and external struggle • pressure • dissatisfaction • tug of war • wanting others to change • frustration

Here are results of letting go: solutions * peace * freedom acceptance * harmony * miracles

The process of going from controlling to letting go may range in difficulty from bumpy to perceived crisis, probably in direct proportion to the amount of control.

THE VALOR OF SURRENDER

The ultimate form of letting go is surrender. Surrender can have a negative connotation, making one think of weakness. But, one of the strongest and most courageous actions in the world is the ability to surrender your outer shell (ego, brain, intellect, armor) and be vulnerable with yourself and the world around you. Cracking this shell gives you a glimpse at the magnitude of solid, unshakable, true power at your core. Seeing this well-spring available to you is motivation to bravely surrender more.

View it as a surrendering *o f* your limitations and surrendering *t o* the profound divinity inside you as a living mirror of what the Universe has to offer. The surrender *o f* can feel uncomfortable because these obstacles have been with you for so long. Unsure what to do without them, you may feel like a long-time prisoner being set free: "How do I live in this new environment?" As you let go of ego, you may feel lost, as though you are losing yourself. Be reassured, you are not losing yourself. The opposite is happening. It is the pinnacle "finding" of your true self and its relevance to *a l l*.

When speaking of surrendering *t o*, you are not giving up to the enemy. You are surrendering to the forgotten belief that you are one with all the Universe. You can reactivate this belief to find what you are looking for. But, instead of "making" it happen, allow it.

Surrender and forgiveness are similar, in that the only way to understand them intimately is to experience them. They are big-picture pieces to the puzzle of our evolution as humans. There are unlimited ways of learning this. Keep yours eyes open to them. Here is one unexpected lesson of surrender from my personal experience:

One night our family reached a mini-crisis point with an ongoing problem in our home. My previous attempts at solutions were unsuccessful. Nevertheless, I started out (as was usual) wanting to be the expert with all the answers. It was common for me to want to fix everything and everyone around me. This is not possible (nor advisable, by the way), which led to my frustration. This time my husband stepped in very strongly with his solution. My ego rebelled, wanting to defend the part of me that could not solve the problem before now. I noticed ego. I felt it wanting to fight. I also felt an internal crisis of holding onto ego's unreasonable will vs. letting it go. I noticed all this happening simultaneously. Keeping quiet, I listened both to my internal dialogue as an objective observer might and to my husband's voice as well. I observed his strength and conviction.

This time, instead of a bullheaded attempt to try even harder to accomplish the impossible, something deep inside me shifted. I was able to detach and see my ego / pride behavior, listen to my dear husband's voice of reason, and allow a wisdom to surface, a wisdom that had previously been drowned out by stubborn ego wanting to be right. The soul part of me knew it was better to be open than to keep fighting to be right. I let go of the ego part of me and felt the surrender. It did not feel like *defeat* or *giving in* or anything negative. It felt like giving up something stagnant that needed to go. My husband felt it too.

This event (this shift), although subtle, was very powerful. It affected each of us. It all transpired within minutes, after a life-time leading up to it; yet afterwards everything felt different. Surrendering cleared out a big pile of old psychic / emotional debris in my way and prompted my husband to *s h i n e*. A lighthearted humor followed. He started doing kind of a victory celebration, proclaiming, "There has been a shift in power!" Our two young boys defended my old ego by saying, "You can't treat Mom that way." And I, grabbing a white dish towel from the kitchen, waved it high, pretending to go down with my ship.

The scene was amazing. The boys were excited. We all

laughed. Family dynamics are so interesting. There truly had been a shift in power, one that needed to happen. He was strong enough to take on my unruly ego, and I was brave enough to be vulnerable and surrender. The rewards for all of us included: more of a relationship balance in our home, more peace and harmony, and boosted trust in ourselves and each other. As a bonus, the problem which started this family story, immediately began to go away.

It takes courage to let go of the parts of ourselves we have become so accustomed to. But, if we can recognize how they hinder us and dampen those around us, we will see the value in letting them go.

In going from ego to soul…letting go to surrender… there is an important question that may be a link in helping us utilize this process. Do we first need to accept and forgive all our past experiences, fully embracing responsibility for them, before we can let go, surrender and enjoy our lives to the fullest?

Affirm: I Accept

Forgive

Allow

Embrace

Enjoy

ACCEPTANCE
a n d
FORGIVENESS

A first step to great blessings is acceptance. Accepting experiences from both the past and the way life is right now brings you fully into the moment. It is a fresh start to move forward. Accepting all puts you in a state of grace, allowing you to break free from the past. This helps dissolve the chains that hold you back, chains like blame, resentment and weakness. Accepting each life situation is a bold move toward ultimate self-care and responsibility.

Financial advice says, "Pay yourself first." Do The Thing's well-being advice is "Accept and forgive yourself first." This will benefit each area of your life, including money. You are probably familiar with the "forgive and forget" notion which may or may not work. It can bring a feeling of emptiness, knowing you should. But how? Something critical is missing. You can be told it is right to forgive, think and say it, but not *f e e l* it. You can learn all the lessons avail-able, but the only way to truly understand something like ac-ceptance, forgiveness, compassion or surrender is to feel it. The feeling of forgiving is one of unmistakable release, relief and freedom. It starts with you. Can you admit the need for and truly see the value of forgiving yourself? This creates an opening in your resistance, allowing you these feelings and the satisfaction that follows. If you can do this with yourself, then doing so with others can be easy and very rewarding. If you are trying and it is not working, pay close attention. You may find that you judge yourself, and quite unfairly at times. Clean up and clear out judgment and you are on your way. Keep returning to the Internal You with tenderness. What a feeling worth achieving!

Any deep and lasting acceptance or forgiveness is an event that changes every fiber of one's being for the better. This transformation begins with *self*. Is it possible to accept and forgive others without starting with ourselves? Here is what an accept-and-forgive scenario might look like in this profile of an angry man:

He walks around with an underlying anger that shows

itself in the form of sarcasm, criticism or outbursts that seem to make no sense. He resents the neurotic people in his childhood for imposing their burdens on his innocence. He hates himself for taking it, along with his inability to make things better for himself. He lives in the past, with haunting memories of what went wrong and the impotent feelings associated with them. If he stays in this victim mindset, he will be imprisoned in that childhood drama. He has empowering choices:

A) He can accept responsibility for being the co-creator of his life. His soul chose to experience what he did (we are that powerful). He was not meant to fix it, but to go through it to learn and grow. What did he learn?

- How to deal with armor.
- Sometimes things can't be fixed, nor is it his job.
- He is strong enough to persevere.
- He only has absolute power to fix, change and better himself, but in doing so he has ultimate potential for effecting, influencing and bettering his world as well.

B) He can choose to forgive himself for perceiving his inability to solve this childhood drama as weakness or stupidity. If he can forgive himself, he can forgive the grownups in his past who were doing their best at the time.

Doing The Thing in Forgiveness =

Forgiving is not something you do for the person who you think needs forgiving. It is something you do for yourself. As you forgive whatever part you played, you simultaneously set the stage for neutralizing distress for others involved.

Trouble shooting

Return for a moment to the concept of picturing someone as a baby. Using this imagination tool can be a catalyst to achieve deep-down forgiveness of self and others. It is not designed to justify past behaviors, but to start fresh from a "good feeling" place of purity and understanding. Try this with anyone you feel threatened by or have trouble with, including yourself. True forgiving benefits your soul at the deepest level. Anything that feeds your soul will help us all.

APPRECIATION
and
GRATITUDE

It is a great gift to have the ability to feel thankful. If you do not have much of it, you can develop it. It starts (as you may guess) with you. As you forgive yourself for any unkindness you have thrown in your way and accept that you are a divine expression of the Infinite, you have reasons to celebrate. Of course, we all have room for improvement, but seeing yourself as "just right, right now" is the foundation for who and where you want to be. Instead of focusing on, or complaining about what you do not like or have, cultivating gratitude for what you are and have now accelerates more of what you want coming to you. It puts you in a position of allowing, which links you with the Law of Attraction.

Affirm: Thank you for this body! What an amazing tool I have, that my soul gets to use while I am here. I will pay close attention to how I treat it.

DOING THE THING

One way to develop appreciation is to notice opposites, a kind of yin and yang perspective. Darkness helps us enjoy light. Experiencing noise increases our respect for silence. When a parent stays home with a sick child who lies seemingly lifeless on the couch, it offers an appreciation of the full-of-life energy the child has when well. You can use this exercise to your advantage in times of frustration and hardship.

Unfortunately, many of us have had more practice with hardship. Some wear hardship like a badge of honor. People tend to say with pride, "I have a high tolerance for pain." Or, "Life is hard, but I am tough." This mentality, like cement, weighs us down, making pleasure tricky. Notice and admit if you do this. Exploring why and answering some of your own questions will get you closer to your heaven. You are not here to suffer. You are here to lift the lid off your happiness and raise your freedom ceiling. It is time to shift to a lighter view. Consider increasing your tolerance for pleasure and decreasing your tolerance for pain, until one day soon, feeling good is normal and you say with satisfaction, "I have a high tolerance for love and pleasure!"

Appreciation and Gratitude help us find peace. There is always something to be thankful for. Even someone in the depths of despair or crisis can give themselves appreciation for the strength to survive. Cultivating this asset brings with it the ability to savor the simple subtleties around us:

the natural world * sunshine * friendship * a bird's song * the feel of energy

Life becomes easier, cleaner, more joyful.

Your heaven is around you. Fear and negativity keep it just out of reach. Accept your goodness. Allow it in. Know you can handle it. Deserve it. Have faith. You learned from suffering in the past. Now it is time to give thanks for all your blessings and the challenge of how much freedom and joy you can allow into your life each day.

F r o m

J U D G M E N T

t o

U N C O N D I T I O N A L   L O V E

And still, I love you even more…
but that is not good enough.

If you learn just one thing about love, let it be how
to love yourself. As I love me more, I love you more. This is
the foundation for human health and happiness. It can take us
anywhere. If you judge others, chances are you are judging
yourself. Practicing non-judgment is a precursor to unconditional love. Doing The Thing means practice on you first.
Trade *critical* for *kind*. Trade *defeatism* for *encouragement*.
Exercise: Look into your eyes in the mirror. Say "I love you."
What do you see? Can you do it? What do you feel? If you can
feel love, *g r e a t !* Understand your connection to everyone
and everything visible and invisible and build on it. If you can't

do this or do not feel this love, you are not alone. Pat yourself on the back for trying. Know love is there. To get to it, you may need to clear out some debris in the way.

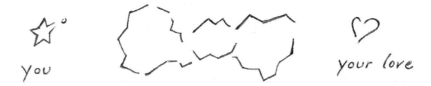

If this exercise is too uncomfortable or you feel no love, muster the courage to look and find what *i s* there. What is in the way? (If you are a parent or are around children, the chapter on parenting discusses how children can help us with this process.) Whatever debris you find is temporarily covering up your true essential being, which is most definitely made of love. Some typical blockades are: ego, fear, resentment, doubt, judgment. Each time you observe and accept the truth about yourself--forgiving and releasing old armor-- you are chipping off another piece of the pile of junk in your way.

Recognizing that you judge yourself and why, illuminates how and why you do it to others. It also helps you detach as you watch others being judgmental. That person that you run into who appears to be self-righteous, judgmental and critical may be:

scared • insecure • feeling judged • self-punishing

• uptight • self-conscious.

Having a mutual understanding that we all experience these trials can bring us together in non-judgment and unconditional love.

LOVE AND RELATIONSHIPS

Isn't it appalling that at times we mistreat our loved ones more than anyone else, as if it comes with the territory? "You're my _____, therefore I can impose my will on you and you have to take it!" …or…"Because you're my _____, you should love me, call me, write me, do this or that for me."

n o t   s o.

Doing The Thing in a love relationship can turn the old divorce statistics right-side-up. It involves self-care and responsibility instead of losing self within the union. Loving unconditionally = clear, pure-of-heart reasons: I feel love.

* We have a connection. * I respect you. * I want to be with you. Those win out over these: I need you. • You love me and have expectations for me. • I need your money • I don't

JUDGMENT

feel complete, so I want you to complete me. (This is the opposite of Doing The Thing and taking responsibility in love.)

When you love and respect yourself fully and do things to enhance who you are (body, mind and spirit), you are making the best possible contribution to yourself and your relationships. Advanced Doing The Thing with love =

At your most peaceful time during the day or night, relax your body and breathe deeply. Fill yourself up with each breath. Imagine the source of infinite love and light glowing within you and radiating from the inside out. Feel its warmth, safety and tingling energy. Let it envelope you in silent tranquility. Allow any thoughts to come and go easily. Return to this sanctuary. Whisper "I love you." Feel love moving from your core outward like sunshine to the far reaches of space and time and feel love coming back from the cosmos to you. Know that you are deeply loved and you are never alone.

13

BEING IN THE NOW

Multi-tasking is highly valued and can be very productive at times in our fast-paced lives; other times it gets in the way. It is time to re-visit the art of doing the single task and fully experiencing one thing at a time. Take pride and delight in immersing yourself in the moment with all your senses. This is where the height of your pleasure and power is. When was the last time you took a shower and really experienced the feeling of the water drops on your skin? Your relationship with food is a prime example of how you can benefit from being present. How often do you really taste your food, instead of the flavors getting lost in what you are looking at or thinking about? Especially in American society, it seems as though the food and drink experience is in charge of the consumer. Absentminded eating and drinking creates a multitude of consumption related problems. Being here / now is a mindful start to a meaningful and healthy awareness of caring for your body. This can mean knowing the origin of what you put in your mouth, how nutritious it is, or simply focusing on each bite to savor the flavor.

Constantly renew your vow to be in the now. Now is a place of information, inspiration and grace. When you are not in the moment, it is more likely than not that your armor is in charge. The past holds useful lessons and treasured memories. The future can be consulted for planning and dreams. But, there are consequences to spending too much time in either past or future. Lack of contact with now attracts conflict and accidents. Dwelling in the past is a place of avoiding the present and is full of guilt and regret. "I should have spent more time with my children." Hanging out in the future can get you too far ahead of yourself, creating unnecessary fear. "What if the economy doesn't turn around?" "What if I lose my job?" Or you sit dreaming and wishing but never doing. These thoughts render you unable to be effective in and enjoy your daily life.

Right here and now, you can handle anything. You can do anything. This is where you *f e e l* . You are actively using your senses in the moment. *Here*, all your tools are available to you. Your Infinite Intelligence is waiting to guide you with updated information. *Now* is where you get your divine direction for moving gracefully into the future. This is the power source. Now is your highest potential for being happy, healthy, free and wealthy. Let's stay here / now.

Do you find yourself drifting too far back to the past or out into the future? Especially if doing so leaves you feeling discouraged or depressed, gently reel yourself in. When you are feeling down...

- Stop what you are thinking, saying and doing.
- Breathe and relax into your body and into this moment.
- Accept and embrace reality right now.
- Look around, notice your senses. Immerse yourself. What can you discover here?
- Find something to appreciate--anything, even if it is just being alive.

In times of trouble or doubt:

Focus and re-focus on the source within, the beautiful, sparkling, powerful energy of love and light that is you. Move forward with confidence in this. Allow it to be your guide, always with you. Relax and release the need to *make* anything happen. Conduct yourself with love and dedication to your internal self and eternal soul.

BEING IN THE NOW

From food to chores and work, to making love, life is richer when you stay here / now.

GENUINITY

(don't look it up...I made it up.)

Doing The Thing = being genuine. Genuinity starts with being honest with yourself about yourself and expressing that to your world. Do you do most things because you want to or because you should? Too many "shoulds" can make you sick. They fall into the same category as *have to, could have, would have, if only* and *can't.*

Keep letting go of things you do out of obligation and replace them with what comes from heart and soul. As you drift from heart, notice the difference in your mood and reel yourself back to the real you. Might people get upset by this, especially the ones you have an obligation relationship with? Yes. Reconnecting with your soul is worth a bit of commotion. It will help you practice not needing approval. You are starting a great new trend called genuinity. Big rewards follow. Each time you answer the call of your heart, you add to the strength of your integrity. This helps you be and have what is right for you. It also adds to the integrity of the planet.

Genuinity may make others around you uncomfortable if they are not used to seeing you do this or if they are not already being genuine themselves. But by Doing The Thing with authenticity, others have the opportunity either to be enhanced by your success or move out of the way. The more real you become, the less threatened you are by others. How glorious it is when we start to appreciate others for who they are instead of who we want them to be, and how glorious when they do the same for us.

How to achieve genuinity: Stop and ask yourself, "Do I say what I mean? Do I mean what I say? Am I doing what feels true and good to me?" and follow through accordingly. If we are all being genuine, we do not have to second guess each other or wonder what others are thinking. Do not wait for anyone else to be genuine. Lead the way for your own good. It does not have to be an overnight transformation, unless you want it to. Small steps work too. It is healthy to be able to say "no" when something does not feel right. Practice on little things first. If you do not want to do that extra favor, "No, thank you." is a nice way to start. If you are doing something for me that you do not want to do, you are doing both of us a disservice. Yes, we still need to pay taxes and take out the trash, but let us weed out the extras that burden us or leave us resentful.

Take the holidays for example; year after year people do things they do not want to do. It negatively affects them and the rest of us. These things range from small to large. Many times there is a falling apart climax around the holidays at a time when life is *s u p p o s e d* to be happiest. If we are doing things we don't want to do, out of obligation--either because we think we should, or because of what others might think if we don't--we are infecting ourselves and them with disharmony. It may look good on the surface, but underneath everyone feels it to some extent. When someone is pretending to be or feel something they're not, we may first sense it as confusing and then either as rejection or frustration.

Doing The Thing simplifies this whole mess and calms things down, leaving more room for enjoyment. Genuinity can save physical health and sanity. It builds durability. Becoming authentic, {getting to know your true heart and soul and expressing it} directly and proportionately increases health and happiness on all levels. With the real you, we all win.

DO THE THING
PARENTING

Do you wonder or hear other parents asking "What is wrong with my child?" Often, what is wrong with the child, starts with the parents. The best approach to begin with when you don't know what to do is to Do The Thing in parenting. This means looking at yourself, Mom or Dad. Instead of blaming, ask yourself, "What is my part in this outcome? What yuck that I need to let go of am I inflicting on my child here?" Examples are: insecurities, divorce issues, old inner struggles. It is ironic how as parents we pass on our imperfections and then inadvertently blame and punish our children for mistakes we make on them. When a parent gives in to tantrums instead of making unpopular, tough-love decisions, the child usually takes the blame and is eventually punished for acting spoiled.

Look at your home life as a family environment. Is it clean, loving and nurturing, a toxic battleground, or something in between? Some children, in conflict situations, try to take responsibility (out of a strong desire to change things) for the adult's problems. This is very hard on them. They want desperately to make life better but are powerless to do so. They personalize it at times, "Maybe I did something wrong." Or, "If I just try harder, I can solve it." If it does not improve, they feel even more helpless. Here is where we see all kinds of behavior problems resulting from the child feeling out of control. Examples include unusual behavior, acting out, aggression or retreating into passivity. Let's not put our children in the line of fire. Do The Thing parenting means cleaning up our act, starting now, so we are less likely to pollute our kids. It gives a double bonus in the end. Life gets simpler and happier for parents, children and future generations.

Over the course of a lifetime, children can teach us many wonderful things, if we are open to learning. Children have an amazing ability to push the buttons that will open the doors to find each and every kink in a parent's armor chain, giving a parent the opportunity to see it, resolve it, let it go and heal it. How does a parent react when their child says "I hate you!" or "You don't love me!"? Close your eyes and breathe. Do not take it personally. Do observe it as objectively as possible. Ask yourself what you may have contributed to their behavior. Give *y o u r s e l f* a time-out to feel how these words may relate to the child in you. Go back in your mind as far as you can for clues. Example: "Did I feel loved as a child?...Did I love?" Self-love is the key to resolving these old traps of the heart. Congratulate yourself for surviving your childhood, whatever it was like. You did it. Love yourself for it.

Allow your children to help you by pushing your stuff to the surface so you can get a better look at it. It is there already; uncovering it brings the chance to resolve and release it. The terrible twos can be terrible or trying or terrific, depending on your attitude. You have choices. As these amazing small beings start to push your buttons by showing you their will, how will you choose to handle these potential opportunities? You can fear the power and glory in them that you fear in yourself and smash them down, which keeps us all stuck in the status quo and adds layers to the armor...or you can surrender.

Let children be your greatest teachers. Learn from them, from yourself, and be lifted up toward your highest good. Children can be our biggest motivators and our purest mirrors. Let's accept what they have to offer. Here is an example from my experience:

Family meetings can be very useful. At one early family meeting, this question was asked of each of us. What do you want the most? Our six-year-old responded, "More peace in our home." That became a priority. In Doing The Thing I asked myself, "What is my part in this problem and solution?" With more respect and sensitivity to each individual, better communication and more trust in each other, I am pleased to report, we do have much more peace in our home today.

WHY WE SHOULD TREAT OUR BABIES LIKE FOREIGN AMBASSADORS.

Parents…step back and *really look* at how you treat your children. You do not have just a little kid in your house. You have a soul in your midst, looking to you for guidance. Let us see and treat our little ones as Foreign Ambassadors in a land that is new to them.

Picture yourself being bestowed the great honor of hosting Foreign Ambassadors in your home. These beloved, highly respected V I Ps have picked you for an indefinite amount of time. They are brand new here. They do not speak the language and know nothing of your culture. These persons are powerful and yet they are in such a vulnerable position. How brave of them and you to take on this challenge! They came here from a place of deep sincerity and good will to learn, to teach and to advance. These individuals are eager and curious and must rely on your help to navigate all aspects of their new environment. They will make mistakes. How will you treat them? How will you handle their mistakes?

As parents we have a tendency to try to own our children (even though deep down we know we cannot own a soul). If we get stuck here, we feel too responsible for them. We incorrectly view their mistakes as embarrassing extensions of ourselves. Mistakes provide invaluable opportunities to learn and grow past our limitations. Let us handle them with tolerance, gentle care and the utmost respect. Honor your own path. Honor your child's path. They grow up to carry on this legacy of love. One of the best things you can do for your child is to find ways to be happy and have a hearty sense of humor. When a conflict is building, instead of expecting the worst outcome, look for a window of possibility for resolution and levity. That is about the time someone may do or say something silly, causing a shift and diffusing the negativity.

Let us be like young, healthy children when we fight. They get mad, tell each other why, make funny faces at each other, laugh, let it go, fix things up and get back to the fun. A deep love and respect for your soul and each child as a unique individual is our salvation.

He's a treasure of a child	*She's a treasure of a child*
Beautiful and wild	*Beautiful and wild*
All his own.	*All her own.*

Mother to warrior son:
If I let you go...
It is possible that your body will die.
If I do not let you go...
It is possible that your spirit will die.

We do not own our children or our mates. One cannot own or hold onto a soul. Hold them as you would a butterfly. Gently hold them in your heart.

ADVANCED DO THE THING PARENTING = A WORLD WITHOUT LEADERS

Let us increase awareness of our wise internal guidance so we can raise children who listen to and respect their own.

They will operate from a place of tremendous confidence. As we become more relaxed with the beauty of our power, our children's power will scare us less. Children growing up like this will not *n e e d* bolstering of externals (gangs, schools, religion, medicine, government) in order to fill internal holes. Gangs are an extreme example of trying to fill a need.

Please notice there is a distinction here between want and need. With the exception of gangs, these organizations can be useful. But, consider what life might be like without the *need* for them. Consider as well, how our internal shortcomings and our dependence on powerful leaders or large organizations may help them be ineffective or corrupt.

PARENT / CHILD BIG PICTURE SIMPLICITY

When our son was about four years old, he asked me this question as he was being tucked into bed.

"Mommy, where was I before I was born?" Good question!

My answer was, "The way I see it, you were a little ball of energy flitting around the Universe looking for a home."

Then came, "Mommy, where will I go after I die?"

My answer, "The way I see it, you will again be a little

ball of energy flitting around the Universe looking for a home."

This conversation ended with him telling me, "Mommy, when you die, I think you will be a planet."

16

TAKING ULTIMATE RESPONSIBILITY

The more time you spend looking around yourself for answers, reasons and who to blame, the more you are relinquishing your power and riches. In the midst of your day, it can feel like treading water, backsliding, being stuck in a rut or outright misery.

Now, aim that same time and energy in a different direction. Stop beating around the bush and go straight to the core. All the problems in your world are solved by starting with you. You are more complete than you realize. You are infused with the energy of the Infinite Source.

Doing The Thing and taking ultimate responsibility eliminates you as a victim. It is eye-opening how nice to you others can be when you are good to yourself and do not allow them to mistreat you.

Most of us have been conditioned since birth to search outside ourselves for truth, to look to adults, parents, school, church, doctors and other authorities. How many children are encouraged to look inward to nurture their internal guidance expert? It is no wonder we get to adulthood dazed and confused. Obviously, we need guidance as children, but all too often we were owned in a sense and our spirits somewhat lost in the process. You are the expert on you. You have all the answers. Always easy?…No!… Sometimes the answers are well hidden because of this old conditioning. It is a scavenger hunt to find your truth. It is normal for part of you to think, "It is too hard" but allow another part of you to say, "There is a solution (in fact more than one); I will persevere. It will be worth it!" If you find yourself lost and needing direction, try this: slow down, focus on your breath. Ask your wise internal guidance system {instincts, intuition, God, higher self, source}, "Please help me get rid of barriers to my clarity so I can see solutions."

Finding your truth is like reclaiming the jewels of a lost treasure when you undertake this excavation. In carefully peeling off the layers of armor, you find your soul, your truth. You learn how to access your power for what your spirit craves.

Affirm: I am taking care of myself in all ways, physically, emotionally and spiritually.

> *If I don't take care of me*
> > *all is lost, don't you agree?*
> > > *Then I infect around me*
> > > > *adding to the collective misery.*

Do you try to take responsibility for things that are not yours? This is just as problematic as being irresponsible or lazy. It is a way to burden yourself and infringe on others. Learn to let go of feeling responsible for anyone except you and anything you cannot change. You want others to be happy and healthy, but you cannot do it for them. When you invest emotion trying to do that, it weakens you and usually worsens the situation. However, when you Do The Thing by modeling care in your own well-being, others notice. It affects them. The effects can be subtle or grand. Change occurs when you are ready. Real change happens when you go deeper than intellect in your understanding; it happens when you finally feel it. We all have our journey of evolving. Let's respect each others travels without criticism. What causes growth? Sometimes change is prompted by a crisis, a miracle, a shift around us or simple readiness. It is time we start valuing ourselves and our lives without a crisis or near death experience.

Advanced Do The Thing with responsibility = understanding that you are upset by others because of unresolved parts in yourself. Furthermore, that person you feel the least connection to and have the most trouble with, is probably the one you can learn the most from…about yourself. Asking yourself, "How can I possibly be connected with someone like this?" is a step toward self-awareness. Being open to the answers from your Infinite Intelligence is the next step in an enlightened direction. Having the courage to drop ego pride and follow the lead of your heart and soul propels your evolution.

You can thrash, blame and avoid (prolonging the struggle), or see these upsets as perfect lessons for your benefit and give thanks for them. Taking ultimate responsibility means accepting that through the Law of Attraction you are a co-creator of your life. As of now stop complaining and blaming and giving your power away. Say to yourself, "Look at this mess I have created. If I can manifest this, I can do something better." You have just reclaimed your power. With it, comes unlimited rewards.

QUANTUM BELIEF
GOD REINCARNATION

QUANTUM AND BELIEF

A dictionary look at *quantum physics* and *mechanics* shows words like "velocities", "speed of light", "energy of atoms", "molecules and particles". A visit with the experts on a show like "What the Bleep Do We Know!?" gives a more user-friendly taste of the quantum world. This world can supply us with boundless inspiration if we are willing to come outside the box and view things in a different way.

We do not need to know the nuts and bolts of quantum physics in order to use and enjoy it. We can learn to accept and grasp its principles at a very deep simplistic level. Quantum physics at its heart is the physics of possibility. It states that we as observers effect (with our expectations) that which we observe. Science experiments show that the outcome and behavior of a subject is influenced by what the scientist believes and expects to find. Belief is the driving force in this process.

The implications of these discoveries are awe inspiring. They remind us that we have the potential to influence ourselves and our surroundings in ways limited only by our beliefs.

Instead of this notion: Seeing is believing.

Try this shift: Believing is seeing.

Look at you and the world around you. It is time to believe in what you want to see in yourself and your future world. You can want it. You can work on it. You can spend all the time, energy and money improving your situation personally and globally, but first you must have faith. Without faith and belief, you are just spinning your wheels.

Take what quantum physics has to show as an excuse to revitalize the magic of your imagination. There is tremendous usefulness and limitless benefit in re-awakening your childlike power of belief. It re-opens a door to miracles that adulthood tends to slam shut. The occurrence of miracles will accelerate as you begin to view them (on faith) as normal. What is true? Is truth whatever you believe right now? We can see beliefs as *f l u i d*, not fixed. Remember, the world used to be flat! With solid faith, build beliefs that will set you free. You affect your reality.

Move quantum theory out of the lab and into life. It

holds hands with the Law of Attraction to assist you in realizing the breadth and depth of your capacity. Whether a problem is in your home or on our planet, nothing gets solved by focusing on a problem with complaints. You can plan for disaster, but if you expect the worst and believe it to be coming, you may be helping to set that in motion. If you believe your problem solving process to be arduous and sufferable, you subconsciously set up a template for that to occur. Then you can say, "See, I was right! Life is a struggle!" Quantum theory is great for understanding the self-fulfilling prophecy.

If you believe your process to be effortless, with synchronicities around every corner, you set up that template as well. Only this time, you will do it consciously, taking responsibility for your past, present and future. You are this powerful. But, only effectively when you believe you are.

So why aren't we all superstars living our dreams in paradise? Generations upon generations have been clouded by a legacy of unawareness, armor and disbelief. The clouds are lifting. Now it is time to set our sights on creative solutions. It is time for faith in this ability. Doing The Thing with faith means that your expectations for a better life will activate that reality for you individually and for all of us collectively.

Quantum theory can help you make sense of your inherent power, making it more user friendly. Your view of power can shift from an intimidating force to be reckoned with to a trusty friend to collaborate with. Regain some of the childlike qualities that give you hope and move you toward a joyful life. Be the observer, believing in and expecting the very best.

Affirm:

I am peacefully powerful. I can gracefully handle all the success and abundance of the Universe, with responsibility and heart. We can all do this. There is enough for everyone. We are creating heaven on earth.

GOD

Once upon a time there was a little girl whose parents let her go to church with all her friends. Each friend had a different religion. The girl noticed that each religion disagreed with the others about who God is and how to live. She felt the antagonism, judgment and threats they exchanged. She came to the conclusion that God would want no part of all this and that religion is a human contrivance.

The topic of God can be very difficult or very easy.

QUANTUM BELIEF
GOD REINCARNATION

It is such a touchy subject because each of us (if we bypass dogma or brainwashing) has our own intimate perception of God, based on very personal factors. We are talking about something invisible and more intangible that the wind, yet all- encompassing. It is no wonder we flounder on the topic as individuals, organized groups and world citizens. It may be our individual struggles about God that lead to wars over God. It makes no sense to fight about God. It is like arguing over the beauty of a rainbow. It does not work to tell each other who God is, any more than it works to tell each other what success is. Success to some is money and status and to others it is peace of mind and happiness.

Most image God in a tangible form based on their personal history package in order to attain easier comprehension-- like the old white-bearded man in the clouds. All our history packages are as different as we are. When it is all said and done, we are talking about the same divinity in different ways. What is the essence of God?

* Love * Light * Pure sparkling radiant energy * Grace
* Source * Limitless possibility * Never alone

There is no distinction between where God is and is not. God is ageless, timeless, formless, genderless and limitless. The energy of God is pulsing, moving and permeating everything everywhere, including you and me. Recognizing this helps us accept, nurture and empower this divinity in ourselves, each other and our surroundings. We can allow it to grow and thrive in benevolence for all.

God and faith are as unique to each of us as our fingerprints. Faith in God means faith in yourself as opposed to some external force. Faith in yourself easily translates into believing in the rest of us. We are all connected, you know. God is who, what, where, when and how you choose to view God. When we tell our viewpoint on God, is it coming from a place of fear or love?

If we gather to talk about God, let it be to share our own perceptions and ideas without right or wrong judgment. Let us marvel at each others views and insights. When we pray, let us pray with faith and love instead of fear. Look for the lesson as both student and teacher of life. This is Godlike. Especially in troubled times, be brave enough to know that God is you and you are God. This is not blasphemy. It is the opposite. A more profound love and truth will not be found. In loving yourself purely and fully, you experience the love of God.

Doing The Thing with spirituality is a journey of getting to know the heart of who God is to you, within you. Find your own understanding of God, instead of what others are telling you. Let it come from spirit. This way you will have a relationship to nurture that will transcend any earthly confines. We can still come together. As we do, it will be from a grounded place of internal strength and grace.

Affirm:

I am a manifestation of God, as is everyone and everything around me. I will express this powerful energy today, to the best of my ability.

A CASE FOR REINCARNATION

It does not matter whether we believe in something or not for the idea of it to be useful. This is true of reincarnation. Allowing myself to sink into the possibility of past lives rewarded me with an unexpected transformation. Choosing to play with this new-to-me idea, and letting it work for me, resulted in a life altering self-forgiveness among other blessings.

My willingness to be open to considering reincarnation was prompted by a deep desire. I was highly motivated to understand and heal my unresolved rage and certain sexual fears, both for which I had no present life explanations. The catalyst for this motivation came from wanting to be a more loving mom and spouse. Prior to this event, when my children pushed my buttons, I would feel an inexplicable anger build up inside. Its source was in my pelvis. {Remember the tiger, and living with a wild animal story? This was part of my history that I wanted to transcend.} On those occasions, my boys were the focus of my anger (expressed as yelling and screaming). Everyone felt bad as a result, with me in a cycle of outdated armor and self-punishment for it.

In my prayers for help and understanding, this is what came to me: I observed vividly in my mind's eye that I have lived a full range of experiences for my soul's growth. Most of what I saw was not pretty: images similar to the battles in "Lord of the Rings", but worse...a dark night of the soul. In my self-judgment, I thought myself to be horrible on both ends of the spectrum. I was a victim. I was a brute. I saw and deeply felt an interconnectedness of those two extremes and everything in between, not just for myself, but for all of us.

This is what I learned. Life is not about judgment, good vs. bad. It is about learning, forgiveness and love. Forgive yourself and everyone. It is the obvious solution.

After this event of observation, awareness and forgiveness, things changed immediately. I was left with a profound understanding, a softening. I felt the power in my pelvis differently, from destructive to productive. I stopped yelling and screaming. I realized the anger I had felt in relation to my boys was not about them. It was mostly about my old unresolved pain.

Your past is history. It is gone. But, if you do not accept and forgive the unhealed parts, it can linger on, still affecting you today. "I can't allow goodness to come to me. Look at me, I don't deserve it!" These attitudes can be so subtle, lying dormant in the subconscious until ready to be dealt with.

I judged myself at first for going into the realm of past lives. It felt uncomfortable and foreign. I told myself, "Even if I am just using my imagination and none of this is real, so what? I am using it constructively to greatly improve myself and those I love!" The end result was a dramatic transformation, leaving me with a deep-down acceptance, forgiveness, non-judgmental and unconditional love for all.

PEACEFULLY POWERFUL

Long before this place and time there was a woman. She was surrounded by war and chaos. Her children were stripped from her. She was beaten, tortured and raped. She was helpless and hopeless. Near the end of her tolerance of it all, she was lower than low. She had nowhere to go but up.

She indeed rose up and became a warrior woman. She got the attention of her tormentors. They were so afraid and yet, in awe. She had eternal power, never to be mistreated again. She said to them, "Know what you do and have done." [When she questioned why they did these horrible things, she learned that the same had been done to them. Their despair had turned to rage, violence and revenge.]
"Now I see you as babies who have a new chance to love and be loved. Go from cruelty to kindness. Enhance your existence to make this world a better place."

She held them and loved them in spite of their past. She gave them what they needed and they left in peace, surrounded by warmth and destined to carry on a new legacy of love and light.

Opening her heart gave her strength, hope and power to transcend the abuse, and prompt a healing beyond herself.

She remains forever peacefully powerful.

QUANTUM BELIEF
GOD REINCARNATION

Since the day Rachel and I sat down to solve that problem, relevance is found daily in Doing The Thing. And even though, that day, it felt as if we had discovered something new, we know it is recycled: To thine own self be true.

I am not first or last with these ideas
but if telling them my way, from my core
might reach a few it hadn't before
and help us all a little bit more
that's all I really had in store.

When we all Do The Thing, what a glorious day!
When struggle and strife and gloom go away.
It is about love, peace, health, harmony, pleasure.
When we all Do The Thing, we'll have these in great measure.
It is not about saving the world, no it's not.
It is about using the goodness we've got.

DOING THE THING

The End…or so you think…

In coming to the back of a book one typically expects an ending. In keeping with my unconventional nature, I cannot oblige. What *is* offered instead, is a *never-ending* hope and a purposeful prompt for a new beginning, one that you create for yourself in your world. And by all means possible…

p e r s e v e r e .

ABOUT THE AUTHOR

Dana is a wife, mother and health care professional. She has spent more than thirty years studying and experiencing self-actualization and human potential. She is an ordinary person who is inspired and driven to show us how extraordinary we really are. She lives with her husband, two boys and feline friend near Seattle, Washington.

To learn more,
visit her website at: www.doingthething.com
or contact her through email at: dana.quade@yahoo.com

ACKNOWLEDGMENTS

Many thanks to my editor Val Dumond, and to Al and Virginia Abbott, the graphic design team at Trio ADS. I am grateful for the combination of business collaboration and human connection I experienced with these top quality professionals.

Thank you to my friends for your interest and input: Nadia, Nancy, Stephanie, Rachelle, Tracy, Paul, Michael, David, Devon, Senen, Mitchell & Reneé, Ann, Sally, Beth, Loretta and Bobbie…and to my entire family for being a constant source of love, inspiration and learning. Jeff, Evan & Eric: you mean the world to me. I appreciate every minute regarding this process.

I am grateful for words of wisdom and guidance from the ether through my favorite Psychic, Liz MacDonald and my favorite Medical Intuitive, Heidi M. Hawkins. This has enhanced me tremendously.

Finally, a heartfelt appreciation goes to Rachel for being the catalyst for the creation of "Doing The Thing."